TRANSFORMING
SOCIETY

melba padilla maggay

WIPF & STOCK · Eugene, Oregon

Wipf and Stock Publishers
199 W 8th Ave, Suite 3
Eugene, OR 97401

Transforming Society
By Maggay, Melba Padilla
Copyright©1996 by Maggay, Melba Padilla
ISBN 13: 978-1-61097-040-2
Publication date 10/13/2010
Previously published by Institute for Studies in Asian Church and Culture, 1996

PREFACE

This book, in a way, has been a long time coming. It has been developing through the many years of pain and stress in our national life.

Many of the essays here were originally written as groping responses to the issues raised since the rise and fall of authoritarianism in the Philippines. They bear the scars of those years, the fire of history still hot upon them.

In spite of its title, this work is not about the task of changing society one way or the other according to an ideology or a blueprint of social transformation. It has not set out to define a platform, and neither is it interested in detailing a program of action. These are better left to historical contingencies and to those with better talents at political organization.

Furthermore, it is not the ambition of this book to set out a theological treatise on social transformation. There is no attempt to be theologically systematic; only an effort to be coherent in our approach to issues that normally surface when the church seeks to be relevant in the world.

What this book sets out to do is to share perspectives, and lessons learned out of hard-won struggle. It is a modest setting out of markers, signposts for fellow travellers in the difficult journey of finding justice in the halls of the great and meeting the face of Christ in our neighbor. It is written for those who are in daily need of grace to walk the path of obedience as they engage the powers in the struggle for justice and humanness.

An Indian preacher once defined evangelism as one beggar telling another beggar where to find bread. This book is in a way like that; it is one beggar telling another beggar where to find bread to sustain the journey towards liberation and social justice and righteousness.

May the God of history overshadow us together as we share in this common bread.

MELBA PADILLA MAGGAY, PH. D.
Institute for Studies in Asian Church and Culture
Room 107 A, PSSC Building
Commonwealth Avenue
Diliman, Quezon City

TABLE OF CONTENTS

INTRODUCTION
Lazarus at the Gate,
or the Politics of Discipleship

I do not like politics. Like many of that generation which figured in the First Quarter Storm of the early 1970s, the white heat I used to feel over political issues has been tempered by years of disappointment, or, perhaps, by the tiring and corrosive effect of having worked too hard and too long at social change with only marginal success.

The 1960s, to us, were a time of promise. A whole generation was raised in the hope that things could be done better. And then came the hard reality of power. By a stroke of the pen, the country was turned this way and that, and the dream merchants scattered.

To the many of our people who live on the bottom side of what academics call the 'great cultural divide,' government is at best a necessary encumbrance. We would rather it remain out of sight, a low-key presence to enable us to buy things fairly cheaply in the marketplace and to walk the streets in relative safety. Centuries of colonial rule have made us wary; used to uncongenial governments, we have learned to carry on without great expectations. Culture and history conspire to make us profoundly uninterested in our daily political fare of scarce bread and unamusing circus. Let the gods have their money and their romp. As for us, we shall take the byways and live as best as we can without incurring the wrath of the powers.

There is a healthy measure of realism in all this. Government, after all, is a sleeping monster that is better left alone. It is too big for us to handle and too stupid to ever dream. There are things in life a lot more interesting: gurgling babies, cookery, dead stars that shine or a line of poetry. The clutter in our lives is enough to distract us for a lifetime.

But then we walk the streets and there are the hungry eyes and the outstretched hands, and the threat of menace from police bursting big and burly with their pot-bellies. Hovels litter the roadside, reeking with slime and refuse, and the smell of putrid air and urine. There are the run-down whores plying their wares, assorted derelicts

1

with big, lonely eyes staring out of dingy halls — the pure, unedited, unexpurgated text of the seamy side of this nation.

What are we to make of all these? Where is God in all this? Where is he in all the hungering and thirsting and the backbreaking and the angry aching for justice and for some way out of the grinding toil and the never-ending wrong that always seems to thwart our best efforts?

Maybe, if we were a little richer, if we had been born in some place such as the United States where poverty is, at least, not always visible and does not meet you in every corner, maybe it would be possible to keep God out of politics. We can sing songs to Jesus endlessly and not have to bother about Lazarus sitting at the gate. Maybe.

But we are not in the United States or some such place. We are being called to be disciples in a situation where the needs of the many do not take the form of loneliness nor angst, but of empty bellies and uncertain justice. It is here, in this land where the small people cannot hope to find redress, where their anguished cry is lost in the dark, that we are being called to respond to a God who takes the side of the poor — not because he loves them more but because in this life power is usually on the side of the oppressor (Ecclesiastes 4:1).

These are the realities we have to deal with. They jump and rail at us, and it is a wonder we do not notice them. Maybe, as in the story of the rich man and Lazarus (Luke 16:19-31), it is because we have become so used to the sight of poverty that we no longer see it.

The rich man is described as dressed in purple and fine linen, feeding sumptuously and living luxuriously every day. Lazarus is described as sitting at the gate, a beggar covered with sores and longing to be fed from the crumbs that fall from the rich man's table. The dogs come and lick his sores. This is the first scene.

In the second scene, both die. The rich man ends up in hell, while Lazarus ends up in the bosom of Abraham. The rich man, says Abraham, has had his fill of good things while on earth; so now he is in torment. Lazarus, on the other hand, has had only bad things; so now he is in comfort.

2

From a purely literary point of view, this sounds like poetic justice. But then we ask, are the rich punished simply for being rich, and the poor rewarded simply for being poor?

The story is curious in that nothing really happens. There is one scene of stark contrast and one scene of startling reversal. We are not told what happened in-between, what the rich man did to Lazarus to merit the radical reversal. But I suppose that this is exactly the point: the rich man was punished, not so much for what he did, but for what he failed to do. It was not so much that he oppressed Lazarus, but that he, in his callousness, failed even to take notice of Lazarus sitting at his gate.

In a study of farmers in the northwest United States, it was found that they classified the world into three categories: people, machines and land. What they considered to be 'people' were their own kind: kith and kin, and other farmers who owned land and were white, Protestant and middle-class. The rest, such as Mexican migrant labourers, were seen as 'machines,' tools for production or farm inputs. The American Indians were seen as 'landscape,' part of the scenery in that vast expanse of land. This kind of categorizing is not limited to farmers in the north-west United States. It is also found among the more affluent sectors of Manila.

Everyday we go blindly in our tinted air-conditioned cars in and out of our subdivisions, taking no notice of Lazarus sitting at the gate. We become so used to the sight of poverty that we no longer see it. It has faded into the scenery, part of the permanent fixtures of our national landscape.

If there is anything that this story tells us, it is the fact that we live in the presence of one another. Human solidarity is such that we all suffer together: we all suffer traffic problems, power cuts, coups, earthquakes, inflation and instability together. Whether we like it or not, one person's deprivation is an indication of the guilt and humiliation of all. It may not be what we have done, but what we have failed to do in the face of someone else's need or degradation.

Part of the reluctance to address the problem of the poor has to do with the general tiredness over political questions in a time when market forces seem to have taken over as an omnicompetent solution even to problems of compassion. On the part of the church, the inertia of indifference springs from the notion that we can live our lives with integrity without having to concern ourselves with the poor. It is as if one can talk about the love of God without in some way relating it to the heartbreaking need that stares us in the face.

I once heard it said with great conviction that it is not the duty of the church to feed the poor; its duty is to evangelize. I had always thought, even as an outsider to the community of the faith, that it was my duty to respond in some way to the misery of the poor. Now that I presume to be in the community of the faith, I am told that this is not really our concern or, at least, not a primary concern. There are others who can address the problem just as well themselves. Leave the dead to bury their dead. Our task is primarily to preach.

I am not a theologian and I have no intention of becoming one. It may be that I do not appreciate the subtleties of this argument. But I certainly do not see how I can operate as a witness to the transforming power of the gospel without having to spell out what it must mean to those who cannot and do not hope to break the cycle of poverty that has been their lot for centuries.

It was Martin Luther who once said that if our speaking fails to address the precise point at which the world of our time aches, we are not really preaching the Word. In the Philippines, at least, it does not seem possible to speak without hearing the cry that rises from the poor.

This is the difficulty posed by the realities of our situation to those of us who belong to 'purely evangelistic' institutions. Is it really possible to speak with integrity without addressing socio-political issues? Admittedly, the thrust of such institutions is not political. And it is possible that focusing on political issues can cost us the liberty of preaching the Word. This, at least, was evangelicalism's common justification for acquiescence to the Marcos regime in the days when dissent seemed a dangerous option.

I suspect that much of the church's apolitical tendency springs from a sense of threat to the survival of its institutions and evangelistic enterprises. It is fair to ask: in our willingness to bypass larger social issues so as to secure our freedom to preach, are we not acting like any other vested interest, willing to stick its neck out on matters of principle only as long as its own interests are not being threatened? In the light of our social realities, can we remain unmoved and still be faithful to all that we are being called to bear as disciples in this country?

The story of the rich man and Lazarus tells us that there is no immunity, no escape, from the general misery and contamination that afflicts our nation. We cannot make a separate peace, retreating into our own little islands of precarious peace and dubious plenty. We are not allowed to find rest until the sight of Lazarus sitting at the gate ceases to be ever before us.

Some will say that we are trying to dig up with our nails again the bones of issues long buried for most people. It may well be that most of us cannot help surrendering to the forces of the market and going through the rites of passage leading to the comfortable, vegetable life of the bourgeoisie, with middling hopes both for ourselves and for society. We wake up in the morning worrying about bills to pay and the onset of midlife desperation.

But those of us who bear the name of Christ are called to respond to a finer, higher tune and dance to a different drummer.

We cannot help but rage and dream again when the kingdom calls and the cry of the poor rises from the earth like a miserere.

KINGDOM
GOVERNMENT

PART ONE

the Church in the World

*T*HE CHURCH AS AN AGENT OF CHANGE *may sound like news to people who see it largely as a moribund institution on the side of the gilded and privileged elements of society. Historically, it conjures images of the dark age of the Inquisition, the violent militance of the Crusades, the colonial expansionism of Spain and of Western Protestant empires.*

There is another story, however, an undercurrent which occasionally breaks into the arena of history now and again: a small community of believers gets fed to the lions for charges of being subversive of Caesar; a band of beggars spreads like a wild romance among the poor and brings freshness to the dissipated foppery of medieval Christendom; a handful of legislators propose to overturn a class-ridden society by introducing a bill abolishing the institution of slavery.

The church in the world, while historically ambiguous, at its best has, through the centuries, served as leaven, permeating and transforming the social order. If, today, we recognize the limits of authority, solidarity with the poor or structural protection for the weak and dispossessed, much of it is to be owed to the quiet influence of the Christian faith. In this section we turn ourselves afresh to whatever it is about this faith which now and again turns the world upside down.

I
THE TASK OF THE CHURCH
Evangelism and Social Action

After more than two decades of debate, social concern is now entrenched as a part of the church's agenda. However, there are at least two errors which surface when attempts are made to define the relationship between the two.

The first error is to confuse evangelism for social action, and social action for evangelism.

Evangelism is social action. This mistake is made by those who argue that the surest way to change society is to change the people in it through the transforming power of the gospel. Sinful structures are made by sinful men; therefore, our task is to strike at the root of social problems, which is sin. Hence, the slogan, 'Change people, change society.'

Although a case could be made for the liberative power of authentic Christianity in people who live out the faith, experience shows that having more Christians does not necessarily ensure a just society. For the past decade and a half, for instance, there has been tremendous growth in 'born-againism' in this country, but so far this has not issued in justice and righteousness in this society.

There are at least two possible reasons for this failure. One is that people may experience saving faith, but may not necessarily move towards the far-reaching social implications of that faith, either for lack of understanding or failure to obey. One's Christianity may be so undeveloped that it has little influence in the places where it should matter and where it should bear witness sociologically.

Another reason is that society is complex and does not lend itself easily to facile generalizations on how to change it. Would that the doing of justice were merely a matter of personal obedience. Unfortunately, there are entrenched powers and monstrous structures we need to address and contend with. There is such a thing as organized injustice, which calls for thoughtful social analysis and complex solutions. You may have an army of bleeding hearts tending the sorrowful and the hungry, and yet not see an end to the causes of the hunger and the thirst. Unjust social structures require more than the presence of changed individuals. Evangelism is not a cure-all, and cannot substitute for concrete redemptive action in our political and social life.

Social action is evangelism. This mistake is made by those who say that the struggle for justice and human dignity is evangelism in itself. To denounce all that hinders human wholeness is to proclaim the work of Christ, which is the liberation of people and the world from every force, power or structure that oppresses and dehumanizes. This rightly recovers for us the cosmic dimensions of what we mean by witness and salvation; things that, for so long, have been understood in subjectivist and pietistic terms. It tends, however, to lose sight of the **proclamation** aspect of the Gospel, the fact that it is **News**, a thing you shout from the housetops or send a towncrier for. It also tends to gloss over the equally important demand for personal repentance and righteousness.

The second error is to dichotomize, that is, to make unbiblical distinctions between what is 'secular' and what is 'holy' or between what belongs to the realm of 'nature' and what belongs to the realm of 'grace.'

Social action, for instance, is said to belong to the realm of the temporal and the physical, and evangelism to the realm of the spiritual and the eternal. Understood in this way, evangelism naturally takes priority over social action in the minds of many Christians. Helping the poor, while part of our duty, is secondary to the task of discipling the nations. Meeting temporal needs is something that all people can do. Evangelism is something that only Christians can do. The one is good for this world only, the other is significant even for the world to come.

In this there is, clearly, an inability to see life whole, to see all of life as subject to the lordship and the redeeming power of Jesus. The work of Christ is seen either in purely **political** terms as in some variants of liberation theologies, or in purely **personal** terms, as in mostly evangelical church communities. There is no longer any sense that all of life, when lived in the presence of God, is sacred: the very ordinary and prosaic act of giving a cup of water can become a sacrament, a touching deed that shall always be remembered, on par with obviously supernatural acts such as the casting out of demons (Mark 9:38-41).

In this work we shall try to steer clear of the tendency either to polarize or to wed in an unholy synthesis evangelism and social action. At the same time, we would like to push further the often repeated thesis that while the two are distinct, both are parts of our Christian duty. We would like to go so far as to say that the gospel not only has 'social implications;' its very substance has a social character. Social action is not just an implication, an addendum to the Gospel; it is an intrinsic part of the Gospel. The preaching of the Gospel is more than a verbal exercise; it is an engagement, a living among men and women that serves notice of the Kingdom that has come.

The Gospel of the Kingdom

What is the relationship between evangelism and social action? Our answer to this question depends largely on our answer to the question: what is the Gospel? If evangelism is telling the Good News, what is the news? What was the new thing Jesus sent his disciples to tell?

The answer is clear enough: "preach as you go, saying, 'The Kingdom of heaven is at hand.' Heal the sick, raise the dead, cleanse lepers, cast out demons" (Matthew 10:7-8). The news is that the long-awaited Kingdom, its reign of peace, justice and righteousness, has finally come. The Messiah, He who is to come, dwells among us.

Kingdom is a political term, and Jesus' messiahship was understood by himself and by his hearers as having to do with more than just the 'soul.' When Mary heard of the good and joyful tidings that the Lord himself was to grow big in her womb, she immediately rejoiced that here was one who would bring down the mighty from their thrones, who would fill the hungry with good things and send the rich empty away (Luke 1:45-55). When Jesus announced his messianic career, he put it in unmistakably social terms: it shall be 'good news' to the poor, release to the captives, sight to the blind, and liberty to those who are oppressed (Luke 4:16-21). His coming marked 'the year of the Lord,' to the Jews of his day a reference to the Jubilee Year when debts are cancelled and property is redistributed according to the old tribal allotments.[1]

There is an obvious political and social element in Jesus' personality and work. The idea that he is king is a provocative one. It is natural that it should serve as an occasion for suspicion as to his political intentions.[2] Contrary to the notion that his is a purely spiritual kingdom, Scripture is clear that he is not just king over the human heart; he is 'King of the Jews,' a nation seething restlessly under the yoke of Roman rule.[3] He never said that his kingship was not in the world. It was simply not of the world (John 18:36).

This social element, quite strangely, has been lost in present-day preaching.

Jesus' lordship has been subjectivized, confined to the narrow boundaries of one's personal life. It is rarely understood that because he is king over all of life, we may have confidence to make every human institution subject to his will and purposes. The powers have been defeated. When we say 'Jesus is Lord,' it is not just a confession, it is a cosmic and social fact.[4]

The process of conversion has likewise been unduly spiritualized. Repentance is described as merely a turning from one's personal sins, and occurring mostly in the individual's subjective consciousness. A dichotomy has been made between faith and works, such that it is now possible to speak of becoming a Christian without becoming a disciple, or of justification as merely an abstract legal status.

This split is alien to the thought of Scripture. As has been pointed out, justification is not just a legal abstraction; it is a social reality. To be 'justified' is to be 'set right' in one's relationships; it is a 'making peace,' a breaking down of the wall of hostility between Jew and Gentile: "...the relationship between divine justification and the reconciliation of men to one another is not a sequential relationship.

12

It is not that 'faith' occurs first as an inner existential leap of the individual... and then God operates a change in him which enables him to love his brethren...These two cannot be distinguished in Paul."[5] As someone else puts it, conversion does not take place in two moves — first, a conversion to Christ, and then a 'second conversion' from Christ to the world.[6] Both occur in one single act.

Clearly, it is inaccurate to speak of social concern as a 'product' of the new birth, an indirect 'result' of Gospel proclamation. It is part and parcel of the Christian message. The Gospel is intrinsically prophetic. T.S. Eliot is right when he argues that "The church's message to the world must be expanded to mean 'the church's business to interfere with the world.' "[7] The gospel when faithfully preached always turns the world upside down.

To speak of Jesus as Lord is to demand subjection of personal and social life under his kingly rule. To call for repentance is to ask people to turn away, not simply from their individual vices, but from participation in the collective guilt of organized injustice. To invite people to come in faith is to challenge them to walk in trusting obedience, to know God in the agony of commitment and concrete engagement in the life of the world.

Truly, the Gospel is more than a set of things to believe about Christ. It is a radical call to come under the discipline of the Kingdom, bidding a rich young man to sell all that he has to give to the poor, or a corrupt tax collector to go and repay all he had robbed. After all, Jesus tells us, what will separate the sheep from the goats is not their ability to spout pious doctrine. It is their constant readiness to visit the sick, clothe the naked, feed the hungry and give drink to the thirsty (Matthew 25:35-36).

It will be noticed that when Jesus sent out the disciples, his instructions had two components. One was **propositional**: "Repent, for the Kingdom of heaven is at hand." The other was **experiential**: "Heal the sick, raise the dead, cleanse lepers, cast out demons." There is a verbal as well as a visual aspect to this kind of witness. The proposition does not stand alone; it is backed up by realities. It is not enough to say that the kingdom has come; such things as the healing of the sick must stand as proof (cf. Luke 11:20).

It seems clear from this that evangelism is more than something we say; it is also something we do. To speak of Jesus is not only to say things about him. We also need to show what his character and his power must be like.

Evangelism as 'show and tell' clears up much of the fog in heated debates over the subject. Some who see it as a purely verbal activity tend to isolate it into a sideshow by itself, simply a matter of preaching and listening. Some who see it from its purely social aspect tend to reduce it into mere social work. In contrast, there is a fullness, a wholistic quality to the growing awareness that 'evangelism is not just a testimony to God's acts in Christ, but a participation in those acts.'[8]

That we need to see it this way springs from the recognition that evangelism needs a context, a setting in which the things we say about Jesus become truly incarnate. The Word must take flesh; it does not and was not meant to stand above the world and its need. The saving power of God needs to be made visible; otherwise it is only empty words.

Context is something the preacher alone cannot provide. For the Word to have a body, the Church and its entire gamut of gifts is needed. The whole Body of Christ is to stand as a Sign, a visual aid to the Kingdom that has come. It is important to grasp that this Body which makes the Word visible is not limited to the local church. The ecclesia visibilis is God's people making the presence of the Kingdom felt in all areas of life, the leaven which permeates all of human activity. It is the Church in academia, the Church in politics, the Church in the marketplace.

It is precisely because the Church has retreated from the world that the Gospel now lacks a context. We have allowed the world to become secularized, and the Church's influence to be narrowed within the four paltry walls of the local church. In the process, the Word has become ghostly, a pale shadow of the Logos who, as John describes, has been seen with the eye, has been looked upon and touched with the hands.

The lack of a caring community that incarnates the Word makes us more and more incapable of being heard. The world no longer sees the big, strong hands that once healed, broke bread, touched wounds and aches lodging in the human heart.

14

This is not to say that we must do social action to make the faith more credible. It is simply to recognize that we are, as C.S. Lewis puts it, 'impure spirits' — people whose appreciation of things spiritual has to be mediated through things material: a sign, a sacrament, a body that needs to be fed before it can begin to focus on things that are above.

We must always remember that we are not talking to disembodied spirits. We are talking to human beings who can not hear us with a rumbling stomach. That is why we must take care to put people in a situation where they can respond in a responsible way to the preaching of the gospel. It is our duty to locate people in an economic setting that makes the hearing of the gospel possible. Otherwise, Ellul warns us, we might simply be throwing pearls to the pigs.[10]

It is clear from all this that social action is not an option; it does not simply follow the proclamation of the gospel. It is a thing that needs to be done if the gospel is to be heard at all, especially in Third World settings. It is part of the process we call 'evangelism.'

It may be claimed that the term **evangelism** has a specifically 'heralding' aspect which becomes obscured if we say that every thing that the Church does is evangelism. For this reason we prefer to use the term **witness** to denote all that the Church does to make itself shine like a city upon a hill. The word carries with it the need to have 'presence' as well as 'proclamation' in our preaching of the Kingdom.

Social action would correspond to the 'presence' aspect, and evangelism to the 'proclamation' aspect in its narrower sense of 'chattering' or 'announcing' the gospel. The relationship could be illustrated this way:

evangelism — PROCLAMATION

social action — PRESENCE

Kingdom *Witness* = GOSPEL

15

In summary, while evangelism and social action are distinct, both are essential parts of our witness to the fact that the Kingdom has come. The proclamation of the Kingdom has a verbal as well as a visual aspect. For this reason the Church must be both a *herald* as well as a *sign*. It must serve as a context in which the saving power of God is made visible. Witness to the Kingdom requires more than preachers; it demands the whole Body of Christ to be visibly present in all areas of human life. In doing so, the Gospel is wholly preached, and men and women are enabled to adequately respond to the prophetic demands of the Gospel.

Notes:

1   See John Howard Yoder, *The Politics of Jesus*, William B. Eerdmans Publishing Company, Grand Rapids, Michigan 1972, p. 37ff.

2   Yoder makes a case to the effect that Jesus could not have been subject to suspicion if it were not that the claims of the Kingdom clearly overlapped with the claims of Caesar. The Caesar question simply pushed to the forefront the conflict of loyalty implicit in the two claims.

3   When actually charged to confirm if he really was King of the Jews or not, Jesus' answer was "You have said so" (Matthew 27:11).

4   "The proclamation 'Jesus is Lord' is a social and structural fact, and constitutes a challenge to the Powers... it follows that its claims are not limited to the individuals who accept it, nor is its significance limited to those who listen to it." Yoder, op.cit., p.160.

5   See Yoder, op.cit.. the chapter on "Justification by Faith."

6   Emilio Castro, as quoted by SCAN, Partnership in Mission.

7   T.S. Eliot, *The Idea of a Christian Society.*

8   Alfred Krass, as quoted by SCAN, Partnership in Mission.

9   Taylor, *The Christian Philosophy of Law, Politics and the State*, Free University Press.

10 Jacques Ellul, *The Presence of the Kingdom*, Seabury, New York, 1967, p. 141.

II
SUBVERSION & SUBJECTION
Romans 13 and the Cult of the Strongman

In times of pressure and disorder, it is usual to hear cries for a strong ruler, for a decisive crushing of dissent and destabilizing elements, and for the suspension, albeit temporarily, of mechanisms for the popular assertion of political will and the protection of human rights.

During the dark days of authoritarianism in the Philippines, such an acquiescence to the denial of basic human rights rested on the premise that order and the preservation of the state took precedence over individual rights and claims for justice. In recent times, the pressure to catch up with the neighboring newly-industrialized economies whose prosperity seems to have been purchased at the price of sweatshops and curtailed freedom, has renewed calls for forceful leadership and strong political will.

The following discussion focuses on this issue and defines it more coherently within a framework of Christian values.

Dissent and disorder

Christians are undoubtedly committed to the preservation of order. However, we see it primarily as the condition for the realization of human values. It is but a means towards a higher end: the free and untrammeled exercise of God-given privilege and responsibility.

The ruler has been appointed to institute order, to restrain evil and promote the good (1 Peter 2:14). To overcome wrong and reinforce what is right, government was given the power to wield the sword. The state is not just a remedy for evil but a positive force for good. The primary argument against a weak state or against the policy that 'least government is best government,' is that it makes government ineffectual, not so much in its ability to punish, but in its ability to do good.

It is in this sense that we may affirm state strength. It may be justified as an apologetic for positive ends such as, say, building a 'new society' or reconstructing an economy. It may not be made a tool, however, for the suppression of critical inquiry, dissent or the elimination of political enemies as has been our experience in the Philippines.

Although the state must be strong enough to impose discipline and carry out its purposes, there are limits to the power a government may legitimately exercise over the individual.

Defining the nature and extent of such limits is a hard and complicated task. However, Scripture provides us a clue in the doctrine of the individual conscience. There is an area in every person's life in which he/she is allowed freedom of conscience: what to eat and drink, his/her lifestyle, in general things which have to do with the sphere of the **adiaphora** — the **things indifferent**, or with questions where Scripture is unclear and undogmatic.

This principle, I believe, extends to the area of political belief. Political thought and belief is an area upon which the state cannot encroach, unless it finds expression in a public action that endangers order and the liberty of others.

In practice, this would mean that the term **subversion** would apply only to a public action and not to a private opinion. Marxists and other such perceived threats to the state may be prosecuted not for their political **belief**, but for their **revolutionary activity**. This also means that there can be no official dogma for the state, a principle beyond challenge and above political suspicion. Democratic or socialist ideals may be useful as patterns for political organization. But this may not in any way mean strict consensus, nor absolute orthodoxy.

Government is essentially applied science. What is best politically at any given time must be determined according to the facts that are at hand, not according to some pre-conceived model. This is perhaps the reason why Scripture limits itself to a description of what the state must do. It leaves the question of **how** to the exigencies of a particular historical situation.

Government practice belongs to the shifting, temporal order of things. It is, and ought to be, constantly subject to readjustment as needs arise and become more complicated. This makes criticism not only desirable but imperative. The vitality of any institution lies in its ability to respond to changing needs and the timeless demands of the Creator. Political practice needs to be constantly challenged and renewed by the changeless norms of Scripture and the particular pressures of a given time.

Dissent, therefore, is not an option that may be dispensed with in the life of a nation. It is necessary if we are to ensure justice and relevance in the running of the affairs of the government. Undeniably, it will involve a certain amount of disorder. This may range from misplaced anger and the muddled criticism of newspaper editorials to the mindless sloganeering of screaming placards in the streets. Nevertheless, these do not warrant suppression.

Whether the old confrontational forms of dissent should be allowed needs to be weighed in the light of the country's need for order. In extreme circumstances a case could be made for the banning of mass activities which tend to be merely disruptive, for instance. However, we need to remember that there is a point where Scripture itself risks the horror of conflict in order to uphold basic human rights.

We see this in the protest against 'healing the wounds of the people lightly,' in saying 'peace, peace when there is no peace.' Scripture rages against an outward calm purchased at the price of more fundamental values such as truth and justice. It demands that the sore point, the source of conflict, be dealt with so that our wounds may be sharply though painfully healed. Confrontation, not the sweeping of things under the rug, is the norm: the coming of the Kingdom itself is marked by violence; discipleship means the willingness to bleed under Jesus' sword. He himself suffered the violence of the cross in the effort to restore order in the universe. The demands of holy justice had first to be satisfied before there could be order and restoration.

This is not to confuse the work of redemption with the task of preserving the world. It is simply to delineate the idea that the Bible does not encourage the ready sacrifice of fundamental values for the sake of order. Order is not a value in itself. It is important only in relation to other values.

The suppression of dissent, therefore, cannot be justified by an appeal to peace and order. Dissent is deeper than the liberal's cherished right to stamp his foot when he wants to. It is the solemn duty of the prophet, of him who, knowing the Word, is bound to tell the king the ways in which he has erred.

The forms which such dissent may take under unstable conditions depend on how much elbow room and democratic space can be tolerated. Concern for this should not blind us, however, to the fact that there can be stillness in the eye of a storm. Moreover, order is to be cherished precisely because it makes the exercise of good government possible. It may not be used as an appeal for other ends. God is a God of order and structure, not so that he may oppress and constrict us, but so that he may allow the full exercise of freed humanity.

The state and Romans 13

The times demand that we recover our prophetic voice, that agonized howl all through the centuries against anything that demeans or debases people, that note of discord in the false harmony of an unjust status quo. Dissent is, properly, our concern.

We need to raise a protest, for instance, against the too facile acceptance of the appeal to the 'greater good for the greater number' whenever the rights of protesters unjustly held or killed come to our attention. Although this practice of social arithmetic is largely a sound principle, particularly in making difficult less-evil choices, we must note with equal concern that the individual and his/her rights are given particular emphasis in Scripture. Prophetic rage has often been directed, not against the trampling of the majority, but against the neglect and exploitation of the minority — the poor, the weak, the widow and the orphan. The individual is inviolable: the dregs of human society can not be sacrificed in favor of social hygiene or a more efficient allocation of resources. The Shepherd is willing to leave his flock of 99 sheep so that he may look for the one lost sheep. From the ultimate perspective of eternity, a person is, as C.S. Lewis has said, worth more than all civilization. We must resist the mass thinking which looks at the individual as a 'multitude of one million divided by one million,' to borrow Arthur Koestler's phrase. The political detainee is, in an important sense, worth more than all the economic gains of a progressive society. His or her rights as a person may not be sacrificed too readily on the altar of order or of economics.

Much of our reluctance to speak, to step straight into the political arena and fight the dragons there, springs from a misunderstanding of Romans 13. Subjection to governing authorities has been largely understood as a call to lie supine as conflict rages in the world.

A careful reading of the text tells us that this is not so. The passage is primarily a **personal ethic**. It defines the Christian's personal response to the state. It is an elaboration, an application of the principle of non-retaliation stated earlier (Romans 12:14-21), to the Christian's relationship to political authority. The submission enjoined is part of the general command to respect authority: "respect to whom respect is due, honor to whom honor is due." It would be a mistake to understand submission here as uncritical obedience. John Howard Yoder in *The Politics of Jesus*, makes the observation that the central imperative in this passsage is **subjection** rather than **obedience**: "...the Christian who refuses to worship Caesar but still permits Caesar to put him to death is being subordinate even though he is not obeying."

This leaves us free to dissent, to question the ends for which authority has been put to use, though we are not free to despise that authority when it exacts the personal cost of such a protest. We may engage in civil disobedience, refuse to follow an unjust law, though we must be prepared to suffer the penalty of disobeying such a law. In protesting, we perform our **social duty**. In upholding the right of that authority to punish us, we affirm subjection as our proper **personal response** to political authority.

That Romans 13 is best understood this way is borne out by evidence elsewhere. Paul's behavior in Acts 16 was far from submission. It will be noticed that there was an insistence on **proper procedure**: he was beaten and condemned without trial. There was also an insistence on his **political rights**: he was treated, he tells authorities, in a way that violated his rights as a Roman citizen. This certainly does not square with the ethic of turning the other cheek and seeing our rights as not 'a thing to be grasped.' Jesus showed the same attitude of protest when he was struck before the High Priest: "If I have spoken wrongly, bear witness to the wrong; but if I have spoken rightly, why do you strike me?"(John 18:23).

The evidence shows that we may have to distinguish between an ethic meant for the realm of the personal and an ethic meant for society as a whole. The wars of Joshua, for instance, would be a puzzle in the light of the command not to kill if we refuse this distinction. Society as a realm for Christian obedience is a different context altogether from personal relationships. Social transformation is within the realm of the judicial, akin to the Psalmist's cry to the Lord to pour out his wrath upon evildoers. We may need to rethink the ethic of non-violence when applied to the ordering of social relationships. The state, in order to function, is given the power to wield the sword. Joshua, in executing God's wrath, had to fight a war. Absolute pacifism is a **personal**, rather than a **social** ethic. To lay it down as a rule for the doing of social justice is to let evil grow strong and run unhindered in the world.

The example of Jesus and Paul gives us a clue as to how we may resolve the tension between our commitment to uphold the authority of institutions and our commitment to preserve higher or more fundamental laws.

The former is classically formulated in the example of Socrates who drank the hemlock as an affirmation of state authority. To disobey is to let the dam break, as it were: the disobedience of one opens the way to the disobedience of the many. The latter is exemplified by Antigone, who felt that she had to fulfill the filial duty of burying her brother in spite of the king's order. The first is susceptible to the danger of totalitarianism: an uncritical obedience that easily results in the fatal mistake of the Christians in Hitler's Germany. The second poses the danger of anarchy: disobedience erodes authority.

Although nowhere in Scripture can we support an attempt to overthrow duly-constituted authority, we are nevertheless committed to insisting on the biblical pattern for the conduct of such an authority. In the same way that there ought to be a concern that the slave-master, king-subject, husband-wife relationships follow the radical patterns of the new lifestyle, there must be equal concern that the structures which God has ordained for society truly reflect the divine will and purpose. This is why we are told to pray, "Thy Kingdom come, thy will be done..." Although Scripture refuses to identify the Kingdom with any temporal institution, it insists that the presence of the Kingdom be strongly brought to bear on the temporal order.

Also, the subjection enjoined in Romans 13 needs to be read in the light of other relevant passages, such as Revelation 13, where state power has become a Beast, an apostate authority that needs to be resisted and dethroned. There are times when power assumes the proportions of an absolute and deifies itself. As the passage makes clear, this apotheosis is normally brought about by the concentration of immense power (Revelation 13:7,16,17), made possible and sustained by the elaborate myths with which every society consoles itself (13:13-15). In the time of Hitler it was the 'supremacy of the Aryan race;' in the recent history of the Philippines, it was to 'save the Republic and build a new society.' We bear with the subtle lies and the deadly constrictions for as long as the myth appears to hold, until one day we wake up rudely to the terror of the Beast revealed.

Like all servants of God, the state can cease to be an instrument of good and pass from that realm where providence holds sway to that land of deep darkness where all that is good in it becomes servant to the demonic. We have only to think of how the entire apparatus of power during the Marcos regime has turned into an instrument of repression to realize that there comes a point when power assumes the proportions of the demonic and the Church must resist with the full force of her authority to speak a prophetic word. As the French sociologist Jacques Ellul puts it in his book, *Theological Foundations of Law*:

> The Church is summoned in the course of human history to speak a discerning word to each concrete situation, "These are the rights of man here and now. This is what man may demand. This is what he needs to be protected from." This discerning word is part of the Church's proclamation. In pronouncing it, the Church addresses

23

itself to society and to the state. It is the mouthpiece of man's exigencies. Normally, the Church should not leave it to revolutionary movements to assert human rights. Rather, it should claim them before man is driven to despair. In the past, the Church had the courage to do it. But it has kept silent now for three centuries.

The task 'to speak a discerning word' remains a challenge to the Filipino church as it faces the particular exigencies of the new political order.

III

UNTO CAESAR WHAT IS CAESAR'S
The Case for the Church as Subversive

History tells us that the Church has alternated unhappily between being servants and masters of the world. Tales of Rasputin in Czarist Russia and the 'Council of Trent' in Philippine political life evoke suspicions of unhealthy medieval influence.

Part of the difficulty lies in the lack of clarity surrounding the nature of the church as a temporal instution, and its precise relationship to secular powers or to the state. The following is a reflection on the church-and-state issue from a reading of two relevant biblical passages.

The two swords (Mark 12:13-17)

The situation was delicate and tortuous. The Pharisees, who tended to be rabid nationalists, and Herod's party who were collaborators and cultivated the Roman connection were, like today's parties of convenience, in an unholy alliance against Jesus. Seeking to entrap him in his talk, they posed the tricky question: "Is it lawful to pay taxes to Caesar or not?" (Mark 12:13-17). If Jesus said no, he was sure to get on the wrong side of the Roman colonial authorities. If he said yes, he was liable to rouse the anger of nationalistic Jews, who bitterly resented having to pay tribute to the occupying power. His response was far too deep and cunning for his opponents to digest. He asked for a denarius and asked, holding up the coin: "Whose image and inscription is this?" They replied, "Caesar's." Then Jesus said to them, "Render to Caesar what is Caesar's, and to God what is God's."

This incident has since been elaborated into Luther's doctrine of the 'two swords,' and, in modern times, the separation of the church and state as sovereign institutions. As this line of political theory goes, the church and the state as institutions have equal power and should not encroach on their respective spheres of influence. The

25

principle was formed out of the state's historical struggle with the church for dominance since medieval times. Since the Reformation and the increasing secularization of society, it has steadily gained ground in reaction to the church's undue uses of worldly power, from the likes of Rasputin and Cardinal Richelieu to Rizal's Padre Damaso and our experience of the INK as a power bloc and of other churches whose spiritual authority have been rendered ambiguous by dalliance with partisan politics.

However, the text, seen in the light of the church's own history, could do with some 'hermeneutical suspicion' as the Latin Americans call it. It needs to be read more 'suspiciously': was Jesus actually saying, for instance, that the church should have nothing to do with politics, as pietistic or quiescent elements in the church would suggest? Does this mean that the church has no say whatsoever in the affairs of the state and should simply go off and mumble in corners about the meaning of its own symbols?

Jesus' own practice would belie this. While he took pains to dissociate himself from the combustible crowds who wanted to make him king, he had among his disciples a number of zealots, insurgents whose political platform was to overthrow the Roman colonizer and to restore the old Davidic dynasty to the throne. In fact, tradition has it that Judas was a zealot, and it is proposed that his betrayal was a clumsy and failed attempt at forcing the hand of Jesus to rouse the crowds and take up arms, initially in self-defense and eventually in capitulation to the tidal wave of popular resistance. "My kingdom is not of this world" was a constant theme invoked by Jesus when both Jews and Romans tended to make of his messiahship a merely political one. Yet, in spite of such protestations, he and his disciples behaved in such a way that they were always subject to charges of subversion, and indeed were crucified or fed to the lions for precisely such charges.

Why was Jesus, and the church after him, vulnerable to suspicions of destabilizing political powers?

The answer, I submit, lies in the intrinsic ambiguity of what it means really to give to Caesar what is Caesar's, and to God what is God's. The untidy truth that Jesus cunningly left unsaid was that what belongs to Caesar also belongs to God. Civic loyalty to Caesar happens to overlap with our loyalty to God. The establishment cry, 'We have no king but Caesar,' happens to conflict with the disciples' claim that 'Jesus is lord,' an assertion whose dangers we fail to appreciate in these days of fashionable born-againism. To say in the time of Nero that Jesus is **kyrios** means to stand against Caesar's totalitarian claims to absolute rule. To say that there is a king higher than Caesar was to relativize imperial claims to deity and absolute power.

This is why the early Christians were fed to the lions. A ragtag band of disciples, they nevertheless found in Jesus a higher, alternative power, thereby threatening the forces that once demanded uncritical obedience.

This self-effacing yet subversive ambiguity in the Christian faith can be seen more sharply in the following story of Jesus' confrontation with Pilate.

Jesus subversive and supportive (John 18:28-40)

In this narrative we see two types of responses to church-state tensions. First is that of the traditional rulers, the scribes and Pharisees who represent that part of the church which interacts with the state mainly to protect its own vested interests. In John 18:28-40, we note the punctiliousness of the religious establishment in keeping ceremonial laws (v.28, the passover) and in recognizing limits to their legal authority (v.31).

The state, it seems, is always happy to accommodate a religion limited to the cultic as in the old totalitarian regimes or narrowly relegated to the realm of private piety as in secular capitalist states and right-wing authoritarianism. The history of Eastern Europe and elsewhere tells us that a religion which does not encroach or disturb the status quo can be tolerated, even domesticated as a kind of sacramental sanction of state functions.

In the dark days of authoritarianism, an evangelical leader stood up a few days after martial law was declared and, from the pulpit, taught people to praise God for it because "now the threat of communism is over and we can preach the Gospel unhindered." Until the very end of the Marcos dictatorship Protestant evangelical leadership was the only church community still in support of the regime.

Part of the reluctance of evangelicals to resist authoritarianism in those days stemmed from a concern to protect the freedom to worship and evangelize, as if it were something a government gives or takes away. The lesson of Central/Eastern Europe is that the Word of God has absolute freedom to do what it wants to do. Paul may be in chains, but the gospel is unfettered. Communism, or any form of state pressure, is ultimately a threat to our missionary enterprises, but not to the gospel. Like any other vested interest, the church is often interested in merely protecting its own cultic and evangelistic interests, removed from larger concerns of justice and righteousness.

The second stream of responses to the state springs from Jesus' own ambiguity about his kingship as being both supportive and subversive of the state (vs. 33-38).

Pilate here shows a tendency to limit the meaning of Jesus' kingship as a purely Jewish ethnic affair. Jesus exerts subtle pressure on him to come under the truth claims of that kingship. To Jesus' challenge to rethink whether his question about kingship was confession or curiosity, Pilate responds: "Am I a Jew?"

Later, Pilate brushes aside the implications of affirming that Jesus is indeed King of the Jews by the petulant cynicism of asking: 'what is truth?' It is characteristic of worldly power to dismiss Christianity as an obscure tribal religion, always rife with pettifogging controversies that are of interest only to its adherents.

On the other hand, to Pilate's pointed question, "Are you King of the Jews?" Jesus also hedges and throws the question back to him. Yet, later in v. 37, he gives a resoundingly straightforward affirmation: "You are right in saying that I am a King." Jesus is both King and not King of the Jews. The hesitation, I suppose, has to do with the refusal to affirm a merely political meaning to the question. At the same time there is clearly an attempt to force the issue as a matter of public allegiance: 'everyone on the side of truth listens to me' (v.37).

This confrontation between a worldly power that refuses to get embroiled in what it deems to be a purely internal religious controversy and an unworldly power which at the same time lays claim to the thought and conscience of the rulers of this world has defined the terms of the crisis between the church and the state ever since.

The tension has its roots in the ambiguity intrinsic to the nature of Jesus' kingship. Although Jesus clearly avoided a merely political meaning to his Messiahship, pointing out the centrality of its spiritual and servant dimensions as prophesied in Isaiah 53, his preaching and practice both announced a platform consistent with the political agenda outlined in Isaiah 11 – the restoration of the Kingdom of David.

This ambiguity means that although, on the one hand, it is wrong to politicize Jesus' kingship — and we have heard of the dangers of political clericalism in Eastern Europe — it is also just as inappropriate to spiritualize Jesus' kingship and see it as entirely in the future.

Recent political landmarks remind us that this kingdom has a present, historic content. Mary's Magnificat tells us that the coming of the king and of his kingdom will mean a concrete historical reversal: the mighty will be overthrown and the humble and lowly lifted up. Mrs. Aquino was plucked from being a lowly housewife to hold the highest office in the Philippines, and Vaclav Havel of the former Czechoslovakia was transformed from prisoner to President in a matter of months. In the sudden, unexpected experience of release from right-wing authoritarianism and left-wing totalitarianism, we are brought face to face with that margin of mystery where all our calculations collapse and we are shocked into the recognition of an unseen power — hidden but present in the concrete political struggles of our time.

The church as an alternative power

The church is a power by itself when the source of her power comes from God himself. The church is an alternative centre of power when she is most truly herself. In John 18:36 Pilate asks Jesus, "What is it you have done?" The fact that Jesus' doings rendered him liable to a political charge says something subversive about this evasive kingdom which Jesus insists is not of this world.

Historically, the church has been a genuine, alternative centre of power when it has been most aware and conscious of who it is and to whom it belongs. There is no need for the church to legitimise itself by state acceptance. Its power comes from above. We belong to a King and a Kingdom which does not derive its power from this world and its forces.

Central to the meaning of not being of this world is the refusal to use the strength of worldly power. Jesus said that if his kingdom were of this world, his servants would fight to prevent his arrest. In other words they would not hesitate to resort to violence.

Note that Jesus at this juncture is past the temptations of the wilderness — past inner cravings for the compelling yet doubtful potential of reformist ambitions, of power and authority and the lure of the spectacular. Now there is only the quiet resolve to drink the cup of suffering before him.

This readiness to take up the cross as a necessary part of obedience has since empowered Jesus' disciples to stand firm in the face of intimidation or the perils of seduction. Bravely they stood up to authorities, and like Peter and John before the Jewish court quietly declared: "We must obey God rather than men" (Acts 5:29).

This first recorded case of civil disobedience has been followed by many more cases all throughout history where the church has been forced to challenge the powers that be because of its commitment to a higher power and a higher principle. We need not go very far down the corridors of history to realize that without the church acting as conscience of society, we would all be sitting in darkness still, languishing in dungeons fashioned by tinpot dictators, totalitarian despots and faceless functionaries robotized by evil empires of both the left and the right. Fresh in the memories of the peoples of the Philippines, Latin America and Eastern Europe is the church as refuge, sanctuary to dissidents hunted down by repressive regimes, the last stronghold against the menace and madness of political powers gone haywire.

At its best, the church is a constant sign to authorities that there is a new order, a kingdom that while not **of** this world is **in** the world and continually poses a threat to established arrangements of social reality. The people who belong to it are on the whole quiet and kindly citizens who pay their taxes and do not wish to disturb the peace. Yet, when testing comes and choices are made in that part of us where good and evil rage in mortal combat, the people of this kingdom reach within themselves for their highest and deepest allegiances and make their stand. It is this quiet, valiant, unaccountably strong and unflinching loyalty to what it believes which has made the church ultimately subversive of all fallen powers.

The church has been with us for so long that we have forgotten what the world was like before its presence. It is important to remember that much of the good that we take for granted in modern life has been part of the influence of the kingdom that Jesus inaugurated. Paul's pronouncement that "in Jesus there is neither Jew nor Greek, male nor female, slave nor free" (Galatians 3:28) brought to birth a new social order that cut across the fabric of a civilization borne on the backs of slaves and saw racial, social and gender inequality as a matter of nature and necessity. Those golden Greeks of our imagination thought of a slave as a 'living tool,' to borrow Aristotle's terrible phrase. Apart from their own kind, everyone else was a barbarian to the Greek and a Gentile to the Jew. Reasonable Romans exposed female babies to the elements in the mountains when they did not happen to suit their taste. Each morning, a male Jew would put on his prayer shawl and thank God that he was not born a woman.

If, in our day, it is at least universally acknowledged that sexism, racism and inequality are morally untenable, it is because the church as a community of culturally and socially diverse peoples has, throughout the centuries, put pressure on existing social structures to be more like the order it envisions. Viewed this way it is, ultimately, subversive, even when it tries to render unto Caesar as much as he deserves.

BE of KINGDOM-VIEWS + PRIORITIES

IV
'THE DESIRE FOR STRENGTH
IN ORDER TO DO GOOD'
The Case against the Church as Power Broker

The church's track record vis-a-vis the state has not been without blemish nor lapses. Often it has been tempted to seize wordly power, confusing the kingdom of God with the kingdoms of this world. In moments of intense spirituality it has tended to stress preservation of its self-identity against the pressure of solidarity, preferring a strategy of retreat and withdrawal over historical engagement.

Throughout the centuries, the church in its relationship with the world has swung from **domination** to **capitulation**, from **separation** to **solidarity**. Domination has been characteristic of periods when the church is in a majority situation, as in the time of Constantine up to the close of the Middle Ages, when the gilded throne of the papacy ruled with both the cross and the sword. Capitulation has been characteristic of periods when the church is weak and in a minority situation, with survival as its main agenda. Separation has been resorted to in times of reaction to its own internal rot and corruption, as with the monastic movement which saw isolation as a form of purification. Solidarity occupied the church in periods when repression caused it to be a voice to the voiceless, as with recent experiences in authoritarian and totalitarian regimes.

Churches in the Philippines exhibit these tendencies in varying degrees and permutations. The Catholic church, being in the majority, wields a lot of influence in affairs of the state, a legacy inherited from the almost medieval power of the Spanish friar. Its most visible representative, Cardinal Sin, uses this power with a great deal of ambiguity: one moment upbraiding government, the next, allowing his offices to be used as sacramental sanction to the activities of the state and the vaulting ambitions of its politicians.

The Protestant churches, being in the minority, have tended to split into at least two types of involvement. These are **solidarity**, in the case of more radical elements in both the National Council of Churches and that growing but intractable segment called the progressive evangelicals,' and **separation** and **capitulation** on the part of those influenced by US Bible-belt fundamentalism, which are usually churches established in the wake of the 1930s when the church in the United States struggled over issues of modernism and what has come to be called the 'social gospel.'

An unpredictable element that has entered the scene is the charismatics, the fastest-growing among all the churches. In both its Protestant and Catholic varieties, there is an emphasis on inwardness and the use of spectacular spiritual gifts. While important for individual renewal, such emphasis has yet to result in the practical outworking of justice and righteousness on a national scale. Already, there are disturbing signs of a tendency towards right-wing politics, either of the 'Moral Majority' type or of the sort that erupts in such aberrations as vigilante groups.

The *Iglesia ni Kristo*, viewed as a cult by the mainstream churches, is perhaps the most interesting as a variant of the Constantinian model, in that it directly uses worldly power to advance its own ends as a church. The modern version of this is the Moral Majority in the United States which, in the time of Reagan, tried to use its newfound influence to further its own pet causes, like prayer in the schools and delegalizing a largely sex-related hit list that includes abortion, homosexuality and pornography.

While neither entirely moral nor clearly in the majority, the Moral Majority is a coercive attempt to apply the force of the law in making certain ethical choices prevail in a pluralist situation where others in the population do not entirely share the same convictions. Like the INK vote, this sort of lobbying is peculiarly disturbing in that a minority seeks to impose moral hegemony over a nation by expediently resorting to political contrivances.

What do we make of these various church responses to the problem of political power? First of all, it needs to be recognized that there is a basic tension between the church and the state which is rooted in the ambiguous nature of the church as both a temporal institution and a spiritual force in society. As an institution, it is easy to delimit its behaviour to specifically liturgical and ecclesiastical concerns, such as saying mass, baptizing, burying, and in general comforting the sick, the sorrowing and the dying. But as a spiritual, transcendent force, it is not so easy to limit what it ought to do in its role as conscience of society.

While, for instance, the pulpit can not be made into a platform for making pronouncements on political issues, simply preaching the Word has social dimensions that cannot be ignored. One cannot preach on a text such as Mary's Magnificat without mentioning the gospel's bias toward the poor, and the tough proposition that a social arrangement which is genuinely good news will mean a radical reversal in structural relations: "He has brought down the mighty from their thrones, and has lifted up the lowly...He has filled the hungry with good things but the rich he has sent empty away..." (Luke 1:46-55).

The Dutch philosopher Herman Dooyeweerd makes a helpful distinction between the church as a focus of a faith community's liturgical and sacramental life and the church as a community spread out in visible witness in all areas of life. Although most would equate the **visible church** with congregations located in a certain place, Dooyeweerd defines it as far more embracing than specific local churches: "The temporal revelation of the Corpus Christi, in its broadest sense...embraces all the societal structures of our temporal human existence." The **ecclesia visibilis** is not just the church at worship but the church in the marketplace, the church in the academe or the church in politics. In this sense the distinction we make between **church** and **para-church** institutions is clerico-centered and artificial. For movements of God in universities, in government and business are just as much churches, parts of the body of Christ bearing witness to the lordship of Jesus over all social structures.

This implies that church institutions, according to their calling, have specific emphases and priorities. The local church has the primary task of the ministry of the Word, nurturing disciples and administering of sacraments, not of relief and community development as with World Vision, or of political action, as with ISACC. Although social justice is a general concern of the churches, the local church cannot major in making political pronouncements, or in economic development at the expense of evangelism and discipleship.

Respecting the integrity of the churches' calling also means that clerics may speak only in those areas where their competence in the meaning of the Word compels their bringing it to bear on moral and social issues. In general, the church and the state are sovereign in their own spheres, that is, the priest may not double up as a Rasputin, telling the king how to rule, and the king may not, like Saul, arrogate to himself the task of offering ritual sacrifices (1 Samuel 13:8-14), or tell the priest how to go about caring for the flock. Each has his own area of competence. Bishops' conferences that speak in a general way to land issues, for instance, or standing up for the rights of the poor or admonishing government of its trespasses are well within their calling of spelling out the Word as it incarnates itself in the exigencies of our time.

It is not within their office, however, to spew out endless position papers on details of complex political issues. These are better left to the laity who, by training, are better equipped to work out the technical implications of their faith commitments. Current corporate action by Christians seeking impact on society and on the theory and practice of their professions and spheres of influence is an example of the visibility of the church expressing itself in secular form. This avoids a throwback to the medieval situation where the clergy ruled not only on matters of faith but on whether the sun revolved around the earth.

Part of the impact of the Reformation in human culture is the freeing of the state and other institutions from clerical dominance. Luther believed in the doctrine of the 'two swords,' meaning the church and the state are independent of each other and are responsible for exercising their specific mandates directly under God. Calvin saw the sovereignty of God as extending over all of human life; Jesus is Lord not just of the church nor of the private and devotional realm but of all the structures of our existence. Modern ideas such as the 'separation of the church and the state,' the Dutch statesman Abraham Kuyper's doctrine of 'sphere sovereignty,' or the renewed emphasis on the regaining of all creation under the lordship of Christ are derived from the Reformers' obedient secularism, that is, the enthronement of Jesus and the displacement of the church as controlling power over all institutions.

35

Calvin's resounding affirmation of the world as 'theatre of His glory' has freed not only the state but the arts, the sciences, and other human activities from subservience to the patronage as well as to the liturgical and theological dictates of the church. The Renaissance was partly facilitated by the realization that one can look at the things of this world **and** bow the knee to the Creator who made good things and made them bright and beautiful. With the advent of the Enlightenment, secularization had increasingly meant, however, the divorce of reason from revelation and the narrowing of the religious life into the private and the cultic, with no relevance to the public crises of our times. In a way, the notion that the gospel has nothing to do with politics has its roots in this kind of ungodly secularism; faith is contained within the four walls of a church and not allowed to influence one's everyday behaviour in politics and the marketplace.

Certainly, the pope may not tell the king how to run the state but the king is subject, just like the pope, to Him who rules the kingdom of men (Daniel 3:28). As we have already said, giving to Caesar what is Caesar's is complicated by the fact that what is his is also God's. Christian citizens owe to God a higher loyalty, which often means going against the grain of acceptable political behaviour. William Wilberforce, for instance, sought to abolish slave trade in obedience to his Christian conscience. He was met with stiff opposition from politicians shocked that he had the audacity to press for morally-based reforms and against an issue that was foundational to the economic survival of Britain as an imperial power. Lord Melbourne, a Parliament colleague, angrily sniffed, "Things have come to a pretty pass when religion is allowed to invade public life."

Like Luther in the sixteenth century, we have a duty to uphold the costly call to a higher obedience when faced with the false authority and hegemony of a church that had lost its scriptural moorings. Like the handful of Christians in Germany who resisted the Third Reich, we should stand fast against the seductions of a secular culture that had replaced the worship of God with the worship of materialism or with totalitarian submission to ideologies of race, class and national greatness.

On the whole, the **visible church** has as its task the entire gamut of what it means to obey biblical mandates regarding the redeeming of society and creation. The twin tasks of **peoplehood** and the **penetration** of society so that it may be transformed have traditionally been allocated to that part of the church which locates power in an obedient community, and that part which seeks to subdue power into obeying Christ.

The theme of **peoplehood** has been at the center of those church communities which seek to make a difference by remaining unstained by corruption in the world, while **penetration** has tended to be the war cry behind church traditions which emphasize the capturing of positions of power in order to exercise influence. In practice, the former has tended to make the church isolationist, a sociological eccentric that conducts its own affairs without much reference to the wider world. The latter has tended, on the other hand, to make the church a power broker, immersed in the wily machinations of worldly power.

Central to Scripture's definition of the church are metaphors describing it as 'salt' and 'light.' These imply penetration and permeation of society. The church gathers in order to scatter; it withdraws inwardly only to better serve the world outwardly. Its calling is to actively participate in the life history of the world, and not to be self-conscious about sanctity and the preservation of its own identity.

It is possible to make an absolute, an idol out of some concern that is of deep interest to the church, such as the freedom to preach the gospel, to the exclusion of equally weighty demands, such as being on the side of justice and the poor in this country. During the dark days of the Marcos regime in the Philippines we saw how some sections of the church were all too willing to capitulate, to be silenced and to collaborate just so they could survive and the freedom to preach could remain unhindered. Historically, secular powers have always thought it expedient to tolerate a church content to be relegated to the solipsism of its rituals and the merely personal and narrowly spiritual concerns of its faith.

Seclusion and isolation are essentially ahistorical. In times of repression, the church, especially, has responsibility to 'open your mouth for the dumb' (Proverbs 31:8), to become a voice for those who have been rendered voiceless or dumped in the wilderness by the savageries of our time.

At the same time, we always need to keep before our eyes the fact that there is a corrupting element to what the novelist J.R.R.Tolkien calls 'the desire for strength in order to do good.' Like the magician Saruman in Tolkien's *Lord of the Rings*, all arbitrary despots start by wanting power in order to do good, quickly and decisively. We know where this sort of thinking has taken us. No one, including the church, can remain uncorrupted by the desire for power, even if it be for ends loftier than the usual garden variety promises of politicians.

For this reason, the tendency of churches to wield direct political power in order to further, not the cause of justice and righteousness in this country, but their own interests as churches, is particularly disturbing. A church that has become a lobby, a pressure group that fights merely for its own moral or ecclesiastical ends, is in this sense no more than just another vested interest, to be fought and resisted in much the same way that economic vested interests need to be resisted when they begin to skew and subvert such critical elements of our national life as our democractic processes.

The church has no need to play politics in order to wield influence. Simply by being itself, by being true to the power of its convictions and the purity of its purpose, it has power. Its authority lies in its own capacity to persuade others to believe in the integrity of its own propaganda, not in the acquisition of political clout by descending to the level of a power bloc.

THINK ABOUT THE OTHER

No POLITICS NEEDED To TRANSFORM

PART TWO

transforming Society: some approaches

*T*HE CURRENT RECOVERY *of the sense that the gospel has cosmic and social dimensions confronts us with a practical question: how do we go about transforming a society steeped in hard injustice and abject deprivation? What does the ethic of Jesus have to say in a context of complex political choices? What is the nature of our involvement in the political and social life of our time?*

Christians of various persuasions have tried to answer these questions. Responses have ranged from **separatist** *models such as monastic communities to* **solidarity** *models such as modern revolutionary struggles associated with liberation theology. Often the church swings from being communities self-consciously seeking to be different as with the early Anabaptists and being itself the center of worldly power as in the time of Constantine and medieval papacy. Christians in rich countries emphasize 'simple lifestyle' as a response to worldwide hunger while those in the 'Third World' stress 'prophetic witness' to those in authority.*

What options are open to us as we seek to incarnate the liberating power of our faith in a situation where organised injustice requires more than individual righteousness? The following is a survey of approaches the church has taken in the past and some contemporary indications of the complex problem of social transformation.

V
THE CITY ON THE HILL
Community as a Way to Change

Central to all traditions of Christian social involvement is the self-understanding that the church is 'salt' and 'light,' a city set on a hill before a watching world. As 'salt,' we penetrate society and act as a preservative against social putrefaction, restoring and affirming whatever is good and just and lovely in the things around us (Philippians 4:8). As 'light,' we stand before forces of darkness, a 'sign' of the truth about the human condition and the meaning and direction of history and existence. We bear witness, not only by what we do, but more by what we are, a redeemed people whose personal sanctity and corporate dealings reflect God's own concern for justice and righteousness in the world.

Scripture's emphasis on identity, on who we are and to whom we belong, rightly cautions many against being caught up in movements that bear only a superficial resemblance to concerns of the kingdom. The exigencies of a highly organized society are such that political choices are rarely simple and unambiguous. To identify fully with a certain ideological line, a political party or platform conditions the church historically and blunts its prophetic edge when it is time to speak critically. As John Howard Yoder puts it, "The Church must not be caught up with the surface meaning of events and say, 'Behold, here is the Christ!' She must discern God at work in history, but carefully, so as not to tie up the Church to the merely expedient."

This concern for a distinct witness to the concrete presence of the kingdom has led many branches of the church to forming communities separate from ordinary structures of society. In the Middle Ages St. Francis of Assisi, in reaction to the dissolute opulence of the church, founded a joyous community of mendicants who roamed the streets with the innocent abandon of lilies of the field, forerunners of the romantic movement and the impulse to be a 'church among the poor.' In the religious and social ferment of the sixteenth century,

41

Anabaptists refused to cooperate with the state and renounced participation in war, retreating under persecution into self-contained communities regulated by a strict behavioral code deemed to be sociological equivalents of what it means to live for God.

At their best, such communities have been signs of the encroaching presence of the kingdom, stubbornly resilient in the face of worldly power and by their very powerlessness becoming a force for good that rivals established power. The strongest examples were the early Christian communities, described, for instance, as having all things in common: "they sold their possessions and goods and distributed them to all as any had need" (Acts 2:45), a kind of primitive communism that has never been realized by modern socialist experiments. Peter before the Jewish Senate, saying, "We must obey God rather than men," relativised the once-absolute authority of the deified Caesars, exposing the fledgling church to charges of being subversive even when its founder had repeatedly said that 'My kingdom is not of this world.' It is a historical irony that the church was perceived as a threat to the established order when it was at its weakest and most suspicious of earthly powers.

It would seem that where the church has been in a minority situation, functioning outside the structures of power, it has tended to be most concerned with simply being itself, a community conscious of peoplehood before God and of the calling to 'come out and be separate.' Where there has been success in being faithful to both the corporate and individual demands of the faith, it has become an alternative center of power, changing the surrounding society by the mere fact of what it is, a beacon of the coming kingdom of justice and righteousness. The Jew-Gentile crisis, for instance, led to communities where barriers of race and sex and class collapsed before the compelling force of being one in Christ. This blurring of boundaries cut across the social fabric of Judaeo and Greco-Roman cultures, premised as they were on racial and masculine superiority and slavery as economic necessity. It was not long before such a civilization crumbled under the weight of its own decadence and the pressures of a minority religion whose social practice challenged its foundations.

Communities of the King such as the Early Church show how the fervent obedience of a small band of earnest disciples can constitute a challenge to secular powers. While not directly conflictive, discipleship that takes seriously the ethic of Jesus has a cutting edge that slashes through the social rot. Mostly working class and operating in a context of political absolutism, the early Christians were not in a position to oppose Caesar. Nevertheless, thorough faithfulness to the social vision of being in Christ eroded the status quo and moved society through history to its current place — past the cotton fields and black servitude of Alabama, Martin Luther King's civil rights movement and William Wilberforce's valiant fight for the abolition of slavery as an institution.

Assessment

The emphasis on community as counterculture remains a major strategy for changing society among traditionally peaceful churches such as the Quakers and the Mennonites, and recently has experienced a boost with the recovery in the West of pluralized discipleship. The emergence of the Jesus people and other such variants of the counter-culture movements of the 1960's raised once again notions of spiritually earnest communities making an impact on the greater society. Today, groups such as Sojourners among the urban poor of Washington, D.C., Corrymeela in Northern Ireland, some charismatic churches in inner-city London and basic christian communities (BCCs) in Catholic countries such as the Philippines and Latin America attest to the power of a community actively involved in living out the social implications of Christ's teaching.

However, community as a model for social change has had its own problems in the past. Separatism as expressed in enclosed communities has a way of degenerating into a tightly-repressive legalism. As with the Pharisees who believed that the kingdom would come if the Jews could only keep the Law for one day, boundary-keeping or the maintenance of certain sociological signs of conformity becomes more of an occupation than substantive isues of law and justice. Punctilious keeping of legalistic details ('you tithe dill and cummin,' things that were not even prescribed by the Law) substitutes for obedience to the greater call to love God and one's neighbor ('you have neglected weightier matters of the Law').

Contemporary evangelical concern to preserve self-identity is somewhat akin to this. Often it tends to loom larger than the more basic need to stand in solidarity with the poor, especially in a situation where to act would mean becoming fellow travellers with those whose ideological underpinnings we may not be altogether comfortable with.

Also, a Christian community is just as vulnerable to contamination. The idea that 'more Christians means a better society' glosses over the fact that believing people may have their blind spots, as with the old ruling class of South Africa who were mostly Dutch Reformed Christians. The parable of the wheat and the tares reminds us of how evil is so inextricably linked with the good: the kingdom of light and the kingdom of darkness are growing closely together, assigned to the same territory. There is no corner of the earth where, like the Essenes, we can retreat in isolated purity. The world is too much with us to be left behind.

Moreover, the church community is not synonymous with the kingdom. The church is a human institution as mixed as our own nature, while the kingdom is a transcendent entity in human history that is both a continual critique and a creative force that makes things new. While a human community can become a sign of its incarnate presence, it is not identical with it.

A strong point of this tradition, however, is the stringent adherence to the ethic of nonviolence even while it advocates resistance. Believing that the ethic of Jesus is normative in its substance although not in its form (that is, to follow Jesus is not to be celibate, leading a pastoral life, footloose and itinerant as the Franciscans, but to make concrete in every age the meaning of his death and the power of his resurrection), we are to rely on the redeeming and reconciling power of the cross and not on arms, trusting in his living presence as an incalculable force that can tilt the balance of power towards the good. Again Yoder: "Between the absolute **agape** which lets itself be crucified, and **effectiveness** (which it is assumed will usually need to be violent) the resurrection forbids us to choose, for in the light of resurrection crucified agape is not **folly** (as it seems to the Hellenizers to be) and **weakness** (as the Judaizers believe) but the wisdom and power of God (1 Corinthians 1:22-25)."

The refusal to use force as the primary instrument for change is something we need to take seriously whenever society is *in extremis* and there are pressures towards violence as an option. Part of the life of faith is to believe that even here, in a realm where other powers seem entrenched, Jesus reigns and is able to turn the tables and win power out of weakness. The inbreaking Kingdom opens up history, blasts through windowless social systems, and creates options where none save the use of violence seemed possible. Our 'people power' experience at EDSA and the relatively bloodless uprisings that led to the collapse of monolithic regimes in Eastern Europe witness to the mysterious power of vulnerability combined with the moral invincibility of a just cause.

POWER IN WEAKNESS TO TRANSFORM

VI
THE IDEA OF CHRISTENDOM
Building a Christian Cultural Consensus

In contrast to the profound distrust of power which characterised Anabaptist communities, churches within the Reformed tradition place considerable hope in power structures influenced by Christian ideas. Instead of a separate community shining as light in a dark and corrupt world, this tradition stresses making Christian principles dominant as a framework for organizing society.

Responding to secularist notions of society which tend to privatize religion, this model explicitly seeks to recapture in public life the influence Christianity had in human culture before it retreated into a compartmentalized and pietistic faith narrowed within the four walls of a church. Political action is a major feature, as well as 'making every thought captive to obey Christ' in all areas of life.

Christian political action, as understood by this tradition, is not so much putting Christians into public office as the effective use of Christian principles in bringing society back to God's original purposes. As a Reformed thinker puts it, "Christian political life is not the accepted political life of the time being accomplished by Christian individuals; it is doing the will of God as revealed in Holy Scriptures in the political sphere of human society." This 'doing of the will of God' is not a monopoly of Christians. As Jacques Maritain explains, "there is a distinction between political activity as exercised by Christians and political activity as inspired by Christian principles. The latter does not need all Christians, or only Christians, but only those Christians who have a certain philosophy of the world, of society and modern history and such non-Christians as recognize more or less completely the cogency of this philosophy."

Ultimately, what matters is the recognition of the Christian concept of the state and of its power in the national conscience. The acknowledgement of Jesus' lordship in the political arena is more effective than the placement of some isolated Christians into office. The ousting of Jimmy Carter from the presidency of the United States,

46

although perhaps one of their most technically competent presidents who was at the same time sensitive to human rights and other issues close to the Third World, is a sad example of how a sincere Christian can be overturned by pragmatic secularist politics. It is this awareness of the power of social climate and structures which is behind T.S. Eliot's idea of a christian society:

> "What the rulers believed would be less important than the beliefs to which they would be obliged to conform. And a skeptical or indifferent statesman, working with a Christian frame, might be more effective than a devout Christian statesman obliged to conform to a secular frame... It is not primarily the Christianity of statesmen that matters, but their being confined, by the traditions and temper of the people which they rule, to a Christian framework within which to realise their ambitions."

The concern for influence in secular culture puts stress on developing a Christian mind, a worldview that could interact with secular worldviews and ideologies. For this reason, the stablishing of schools where minds can be trained to integrate biblical perspectives into the theory and practice of professional disciplines is given heavy emphasis. Likewise, the capturing of people's minds and imaginations through art and the media, the academia, and other channels of public debate is a part of this tradition.

The reality of living in a complex fallen world opens this model to the possibility of a 'just war' under certain circumstances. Unlike absolute pacifism, it recognises the necessity of defense and the pressure of making tragic choices when to do so would mean less-evil consequences. Power is to be used, subdued into a servant for good. There is no virtue in powerlessness.

Unlike the emphasis on community which hopes to influence primarily by example, this kind of social involvement seeks change mostly by an appeal to power structures. It involves the articulation of a vision of society based on what has been called 'creational ordinances,' and the critiquing of presuppositions behind the prevailing

47

political culture. In our context, this means coming up with political alternatives, with a programme of action based on clear biblical perspectives, and not merely reacting to other people's agendas or deciding whether to join existing movements. It means working out a biblical framework for understanding such issues as globalization, land reform, national debt and market economy, environmentalism, or nationalism and imperialism. It will require corporate action that addresses itself to Congress and the mechanisms of government as well as propaganda work aimed at the popular imagination.

In its older form, we see this tradition operating in predominantly Catholic cultures such as the Philippines and Latin America, where remnants of the church's medieval power remains, an historical residue that is sometimes useful as a counterforce to oppressive authoritarianism. Progressive elements in the hierarchy in Latin America or the Catholic leadership in this country at the height of the crisis at EDSA have served as buffer against forces of oppression. This seems to work, however, only in a situation where the church is in the majority, and has power to influence political decisions because of a long tradition of entrenchment.

The more recent form of this approach is seen in Europe in the work of the statesman Abraham Kuyper, who founded the Anti-Revolutionary Party, and the legacy of Francis Schaeffer; both reacted to liberal humanist ideas of the French Revolution and had, as capital, centuries of Christian tradition. A rabid variant is the aggressive public profile of the religious right in America, who have distorted the call to put faith once again into the marketplace into a battle-cry for the reassertion of narrowly-selected Christian values based on the United States' faith inheritance defined as the 'Protestant work ethic' and Jeffersonian libertarianism.

Assessment

The current focus on the comprehensiveness of Jesus' redemptive and creative work owes much to the work of those who seek to reconstruct that great architectonic structure called 'Christendom.' The return of the sense that Jesus is Lord even of the marketplace has led to renewed visions of a relevant Christianity making an impact and transforming sick societies. Leavening power structures with the ethos of the Kingdom is certainly a major agenda in the face of such 'new demons' as organised injustice, runaway technology and market forces and triumphalist ideologies.

However, this model's confidence in power as a force for good has a tendency to slip into a Constantinian model of going about the King's business. Until fairly recently, the church has been largely identified with the status quo, an alliance of power that seems to be endemic to the idea of the church wielding political influence. A modern example of the distortion that arises from this is the triumphalist politics of the Moral Majority in the United States, which has not hesitated to use coercive tools of public persuasion.

It is true, of course, that Christian values, if they are rooted in creation, have a significance that is not limited to those who listen to them. There is a need to maintain radical suspicion, however, of the way power is put to the service of advancing our agenda. It is tragic, for instance, the way the resurgent religious right in the United States has forged a kind of church/state fusion, with the political powers gaining religious sanction from a church uncritical of the political system to which it is attached, and the church making use of political authority to impose its own moralistic views on a religiously pluralistic majority.

Also, the idea of a 'new Christendom' is susceptible to confusing christianized structures or cultures as God's visible kingdom on earth. In baptizing democratic capitalism as continuous with its Christian heritage, 'culture Christianity' such as that of the religious right in the United States runs the danger of repeating the pious militancy of the Crusades, mistaking the cause of the kingdom with the aggressive promotion of a merely ideological vision, perceiving the loss of christian cultural hegemony in secular and socialist societies as somehow equivalent to an apostasy worth waging a *jihad* for.

A shining feature of this model, however, is its emphasis on the lordship of Jesus over all structures. It has raised again the importance of the laity, and the concern that biblical insight should not remain the preserve of the specialist. It has recovered for us the

49

critical need for the gifts and resources of the whole Church, and for developing thoroughly renewed minds that are able to enter the sphere of secular debate and integrate biblical ideas into its discussions. Usually, those with communication skills at the forefront of today's ideological battles are either undeveloped as Christians or inept as politicians. For social involvement to become biblically informed, practitioners in such fields as media, politics, or the sciences as a whole must be able to combine disciplined analysis and political sophistication with theological literacy.

Concretely, this model calls for movements of christians engaged in 'cultural work,' that is, transforming values through raising consciousness of biblical themes as they apply to society. It means academics thinking through the contextual social equivalents of what the Bible means by transformation and artists articulating the christian social vision imaginatively. It means organizing reflection fellowships along professional lines and engaging in political advocacy wherever pressure is necessary to effect changes in policy. All in all, this model belongs to that category of ministry which, in the language of the parable of the sower, is 'preparing the soil,' softening the hard ground of established competing ideologies and religious systems and creating a climate where the seed of the Word can be understood and take root.

CONVERSON | EVANGELISM TO CREATE A REPRESENTATION OF GOD'S KINGDOM ON EARTH, AS GOD INTENDED, BUT TO BE CONFUSED w/ THE ACTUAL KINGDOM OF GOD.

VII
THE GOSPEL OF LIBERATION
Restructuring Power Relations

A Third World model that has risen out of an acute sense of the 'underside of history' — that view from the side of the poor who get swept to the sidelines in spite of their history-making size — is the liberationist emphasis on solidarity with the oppressed in their struggle to release themselves from the iron grip of unjust power relations. This form of social involvement puts a great deal of stress on the structural nature of poverty and injustice, and the need to redress social imbalances through a radical rearrangement of the social order. — STRUCTURAL / GOV'T CHANGE

At the center of this model is the realization that oppression is based on certain objective patterns of power relationships, and not merely because the poor are caught in a kind of 'culture of poverty' such as laziness or fatalism or the lack of an environment which supports initiative or enterprise such as that which gave rise to the so-called Protestant work ethic. For transformation to take place, this model insists that objective conditions, that is, economic relations, be reversed in favour of the underclass. As someone graphically puts it, "good news for the poor is bad news for the rich, and letting my people go is not good news for Pharaoh."

Sensitive to the structural dynamics of sin, this model derives inspiration from Scripture's unequivocal particularity towards the poor in its prophetic concerns. This partiality, or 'preferential option' for the poor, is rooted in the theological fact that while Jesus **died** for **all**, he **lived** especially for **some** — the weak, the poor and the dispossessed. While it is true that all are sinners and need forgiveness, **not** all are victims of injustice. The poor are poor mostly because "on the side of their oppressor is power" (Ecclesiastes 4:1). There is none to comfort them but the God who, according to the prophets, rages against those "who sell the righteous for silver, and the needy for a pair of shoes — they that trample the head of the poor into the dust of the earth, and turn aside the way of the afflicted" (Amos 2:6-7).

51

God is on the side of the poor because, in this earth, power structures are usually biased against them.

Solidarity with the poor, in the more extreme forms of this model,
is defined concretely as participation in class struggles. It emphasizes
praxis, or concrete historical engagement, as primary means of
knowing God and the world. The kingdom moves, not only within
the internal structures of the church, but in the liberation struggles
and humanizing efforts of secular movements.

Deriving its paradigms from the Exodus and Jesus' messianic
platform as announced in Luke 4, this tradition sees salvation in
political, historical and spiritual terms. The Exodus, according to
liberation theologian Gustavo Gutierrez, is an 'historical-salvific fact;
it shows God intervening historically to save his people, an act that is
both creative and redemptive. The Jews were released from oppression in Egypt to become a people and construct a just society; they
were breaking from the old order and creating a new one. In the
incarnation, God's presence becomes a historical reality, indwells the
Christian, and is universalized in every person: "Not only is the
Christian a temple of God," says Gutierrez, "every man is." This
universalization of the presence of God makes possible a complete
openness to the collective struggle towards a 'Christo-finalized
history.' CHARITY WILL CONVICE SOUETY (?)

Assessment

A strength of liberation theology as a category of engagement is its
recognition of structural captivities from which people need to be
freed. Paul, in speaking of the 'powers' means more than personal
spiritual beings ranged in opposition to the kingdom: he also means
depersonalized forces of evil at work in the social climate ('the prince
of the power of the air') or entrenched in structures of the created
order which have become 'principalities' or realms of the demonic.
The sense that we are up against overwhelming forces of institutionalized injustice is founded on the reality that evil has macrocosmic
dimensions. Sin expresses itself not only in personal and individual
badness such as adultery or perverted sex but also in corporate and

systemic forms such as apartheid in the old South Africa or economic exploitation in many parts of the Third World by native ruling classes and multinational entities.

Solidarity with the poor is likewise a major prophetic theme that this model has recovered for us. Underlying this particularity in political commitment is the biblical idea that the coming of the kingdom is to be marked by a 'great reversal' in the fortunes of the rich and the poor. Wherever the kingdom shows its presence, there is going to be a radical shakedown in the social order and the place of the poor in its arrangements. While this is yet to be realised in full historically, any transformation that issues genuinely from the work of the kingdom will have this characteristic even now of uplifting the poor and over throwing the mighty. For the kingdom, according to Jesus, is a messianic feast where the poor and the lowly find themselves as guests (Luke 14:16-24).

Critical to this model is the problem of how precisely to actualize solidarity with the poor. Extreme liberationists, borrowing from Marxist categories, have mostly meant by this engagement in revolutionary struggles, assuming that change in the socio-economic process is necessarily conflictive and often violent. Moderate elements would lay stress on empowerment of the poor through grassroots movements, strengthening the people's political will by the experience of non-violent collective action.

The curious phenomenon of Christianity becoming a handmaiden to the class struggle is an example of what it means to put the faith at the service of certain perceptions and arrangements of reality. If to the religious right the kingdom is tied up with the blind mechanisms of market forces, to the religious left it is tied up with the inexorably increasing tension of the dialectic working out the salvation of the poor through the antagonisms of class-ridden societies. While awareness of the structural dimensions to the problem of the poor requires openness to all kinds of sociological insight, there is danger of blunting the critical edge of transcendence by identifying the faith too closely with a particular grid in analysing the social process.

Intrinsic to the kingdom is a critical element that refuses to be domesticated into a merely ideological commitment. While the 'now' part puts pressure on the present social order to move towards its vision, the 'not-yet' registers discontent, withholds complete identification with any social force at work in human history. The kingdom is not to be identified complètely with existing movements, whether they be bulwarks of orthodoxy like the church, or forces of orthopraxis like liberation struggles.

The concern for orthopraxis (right action) is a biblical theme that antedates Marxism. Prophetic literature resoundingly affirms that to know God is to do justice (Jeremiah 22: 13-17) and not primarily to make many prayers. "To obey is better than sacrifice," said Samuel (1 Samuel 15:22), adherence to cultic ritual is not necessarily an indication of loving God. "What does the Lord require," said Micah, "but to do justice, to love kindness and to walk humbly with your God?" (Micah 6:8). **Doing** and **knowing** are synthesized in scripture into one act. "If you continue in my word," says Jesus, "you will know the truth, and the truth shall make you free" (John 8:32). Obedience, walking in his ways, are prerequisites for knowing him: "Why do you call me 'Lord, Lord' and not do what I tell you?" (Matthew 7:21). The split between faith and works, knowing and doing, reflection and action is a sickness of mind derived from Greek dichotomies and 'essentialist' thinking, not from Hebrew styles of cognition.

The call for praxis, for concrete immersion in the life of the world, is at the heart of the meaning of the incarnation. However, solidarity with the transforming forces of our history belongs to the creative rather than the redemptive work of Christ. While it is true that both are intrinsic parts of salvation as a single, complex process, a distinction still needs to be made.

It is true that the redemptive work of Christ covers all of creation (Romans 8:21) and human culture (Revelation 21:24,26). It is part of the Good News that there will be, not only a new heaven, but a new earth and a new social order out of the womb of our present historical struggles. The world as we know it now shall be transformed into something rich and strange (Isaiah 65:17-25). Social transformation, in so far as it honours the name of him who works for good in all the creative forces at work in society, is somehow caught up in all that God is doing in the world. However, the biblical focus on salvation as primarily forgiveness of sin constrains us to view the work of liberation as primarily recreative rather than salvific, a participation in the recreative powers of the age to come. Structures are transformed; they do not get saved.

Also, there is a great divide between those who are engaged historically because they bear the name of Christ and those who are their fellow travellers because of some common revolutionary vision. In a creational sense, Christ is in every man (Colossians 1:17, Acts 17:28); in a redemptive sense, scripture is clear that he does not indwell every one (Romans 8:9, 14-16). Because we are all human beings made in the image of God, there is always solidarity in Adam. However, because our ways as sons of light and sons of darkness divide, there is not always solidarity in Christ. While as human beings there is always solidarity in Adam, as peoples of two kingdoms there is not always solidarity in Christ.

It is of course true that in the incarnation there is a sense in which the second Adam can be found in every man and woman: "as you did it to one of the least of these my brethren, you did it to me." (Matthew 25:31-46). In Jesus, God has become our neighbour; he is the man or woman we happen to feed or clothe or care for when hungry or naked or sick and needing comfort. The beggar who thrusts his hand out at us in the street is, startlingly, a proxy for Christ.

This universalization of the image of Christ does not mean, however, the universal presence of the spirit of Christ. As Son of Man there is a sense in which he shares our history and our struggles. As the unblemished Lamb of God who takes away the sin of the world, he is the 'wholly other' messianic element that both affirms and critiques our collective historical efforts. While our common humanity may situate us in the same collective pilgrimage towards justice, our identity in Christ makes us wary of participating in revolutionary projects that deny the values of the kingdom and the means that issue from it.

55

VIII
THE PRACTICE OF COMPASSION
The Developmental Model

Perhaps the most commonly practiced among Christians, immediate mercy and relief of the sufferer were also exercised in the old Jewish culture, where acts of charity were structured into the life of the people.

The Old Testament is full of laws regarding care of the poor and the weak. It is forbidden to exact interest when lending to the poor, and a garment taken in pledge must be restored to the owner before sundown so he has something with which to cover himself. A slave may go free in the seventh year of service, the land likewise shall rest and lie fallow so that the poor may eat of its produce (Exodus 22:25-27, 21:2, 23:11). One is not to harden the heart or close the hand against the needy (Deuteronomy 15:7-11), and at harvest one should leave some of the sheaves and the gleanings for the sojourner, the fatherless and the widow (Deutronomy 24:19-21).

In the New Testament, Jesus tells his disciples to "sell your possessions, and give alms" (Luke 12:33), and holds up the story of the Good Samaritan as an example of loving one's neighbor without limits (Luke 10:25-37). He pronounces Zacchaeus saved when Zacchaeus offers to give half of his goods to the poor (Luke 19:8-9). In contrast, he makes a sad commentary on the rich young ruler whose face fell when told to sell all that he had and give the proceeds to the poor: "it is easier for a camel to go through the eye of a needle than for a rich man to enter the kingdom of God" (Luke 18:25). The ability to divest oneself of one's goods for the sake of the needy is clearly an indication, in the mind of Jesus, of the state of one's spiritual health.

Such a focused and compassionate response to the plight of the poor continues to engage many Christians. The history of the missionary movement is replete with stories of oustanding jungle doctors and educators, men and women who have planted the flag of Christ firmly in many lands by bringing wholeness and light spiritually and physically. Wherever the gospel had been preached, closely following it had been a mission hospital or a school, familiar landmarks of the expansion of the cause of Christ.

In our day, Mother Teresa stands as a symbol of Christianity's compassionate particularity — the focused commitment to the needs of individual men and women and not just some abstract mass or class of humankind. In her work among the dying in the streets of Calcutta, we see incarnate once again the Christ who once walked the streets of Galilee and healed the sick and the infirm.

In many squatter communities today, we find small pockets of churches which bear witness to the Christ who lived among the poor. Doctors tread tortuous mountain paths to reach isolated tribal villages needing medical help. Community organizers brave suspicion and the dangers of being caught in the crossfire of political currents to rekindle hope among villagers dislocated by fighting between military and insurgency elements. Agri-business experts relocate to the hinterlands to open up the wild woods and to develop farms for resettling urban poor communities going back to the land. Professionals who could have a career elsewhere choose to serve sacrificially in places where their expertise means something to the vast masses of our people who are without access to basic services such as water and health facilities, farm-to-market roads, electricity or food production technologies. Christian men and women all throughout the faith's erratic history have been ready to lay down their lives in service of the poor because they bear the name of Christ.

Assessment

In general, Christians have been quite good at delivering concrete social services like feeding programmes, health care, education, water and sanitation facilities, and ways of increasing food production and income. These are things worth rejoicing about. However, there is a tendency to be caught in mere developmentalism, and to doing things without sensitivity to the larger socio-economic context in which poverty operates. Access to goods and services is usually dangled as a carrot for acceptance of the faith. The phenomenon of 'rice Christians' is a direct result of the tendency to use errands of compassion as a means to an end, rather than a thing which in itself honours the God of the poor.

The complex nature of poverty precludes naive notions of society being transformed by putting more Christians into office or by a little more love and feeding programmes. Pockets of compassion here and there may make life a little more bearable for the masses of our poor. These may not substitute, however, for the task of addressing the larger socio-economic context in which ancient poverty and injustice are rooted. It was reported, for instance, that the old Smokey Mountain in the Philippines had at one time more than 300 non-governmental organizations working in the area. Yet, as the people who were once there said, "we remain poor." Many preferred to live on refuse for their livelihood because the alternative was the indignity of unemployment and utter destitution. We need to confront the powers that be in their structural dimensions if we are to see the poor inching towards a measure of well-being in this country.

The Old Testament reflects this concern for structural mechanisms that would correct imbalances in the social system. The provision for a Year of Jubilee in Leviticus 25, for instance, was meant as a corrective to the untrammeled accumulation and concentration of economic power in the hands of a few ascendant clans. It legislates for the return of ancestral property to impoverished Jews who may have lost it within a fifty-year cycle. It provides for the release of slaves and the cancelling of their debts. Land as primary means of production and wealth may not be sold in perpetuity, discouraging speculative buying and ensuring periodic readjustments when the economic order becomes unduly asymmetrical.

Faced with the complex nature of the power structures we are dealing with, we have no choice but to see to it that our social structures and our own institutions reflect the same protection for the rights of the weak and dispossessed.

Also, the incarnation provides us with an archetypal process by which to critique our own efforts at transformation. How much of the development going on in a community is due to the intervention and infusion of massive resources from the outside and how much of it springs from the initiative and endogenous resources of the people?

Have we really become one with the people in such a way that we are able to be where they are — seeing problems just as they see them and confronting them in the way they would? Are we appropriating their technologies, listening to their solutions, taking their context seriously in the effort to go where they would like to go?

Often, we follow a **multinational** rather than an **incarnational** model of development. We come in with our own agenda — usually evangelism, with social services as an attraction — and manage to have access into the community by raising expectations of resource assistance and technology transfer. This is the exact opposite of the incarnation, a process where Jesus 'empties' himself of the trappings of power, stripping himself of the baggage attendant to his status as a divine person, and coming down to become like us, humanly vulnerable and subject to the same injustice and deprivations of our social conditions (Philippians 2:6-8). In the same manner, we are to 'dwell' among the people and identify as deeply as we can without benefit of the cultural or social or educational baggage which usually accompanies us in our journey towards solidarity with the poor. This process restores parity and avoids the indignity of paternalism which often reduces people into objects of charity or even of 'empowerment.' We do not do things **to** the poor; we do things **with** them.

The incarnation also tells us that the Son of God became a man, not so that we may become divine, but so that we may become more truly human. This means that our attempts at solidarity should take care that the poor do not end up merely like us, — Christians with middle class values and aspirations to a comfortable bourgeois lifestyle, the sort of 'redemptive lift' that missiologists talk so proudly about. We are aiming, not merely at the kind of development that generates better income for higher consumption of the world's goods, but at the sort of transformation that changes both us and the poor into true people of the kingdom, with a deeper concern for justice and empathy for those who fail and are unable to 'pull themselves by their bootstraps' as Margaret Thatcher used to say.

Ultimately, we are not interested in merely making food drops from the sky for places in famine such as Somalia and other bottomless pits of abject need, important though this may be as a quick response to recurrent food crises in troubled spots torn by war and internal strife. We are not in the business of simply pushing for an economic boom that would land the Philippines on its feet by the year 2000, or, like Singapore's Prime Minister Go Chok Tong, promising to eradicate poverty in the land by making everybody eventually middle class. These, of course, are all worthy goals for governments who deal in the realm of the politically possible.

As churches, however, we are ultimately in the business of both fattening and healing our land, of seeing new men and women transforming and liberating themselves and the larger society in those places where the powers that be have established strongholds of poverty, oppression and bitter enmity. We are aiming for the length and breadth of **shalom**, for that seamless wholeness in all that makes us fully human as embodied for us by the Son of Man.

IX

PROPHET, PRIEST, KING
Some Suggested Roles for the Church

It would seem that the church in its social involvement vis-a-vis the secular powers has tended to swing between power and powerlessness, separation and solidarity. Some parts emphasize social compassion, others social construction. Factors that have shaped its responses had to do mainly with its relative size and strength at any given period and the level of theological sensitivity to cosmic and structural dimensions of the gospel, with a degree of concern for self-identity on the hand and solidarity with the poor on the other.

In the following discussion, we shall attempt to integrate all these approaches from the standpoint of being sharers in Christ's messianic office of prophet, priest, and king.

THE PROPHETIC OFFICE
Bringing the Word of God to the world.

The Church as conscience to society subjects society to profound scrutiny: to what depth is the foundation of our society not merely neutral but positively anti-Christian? Because of access to the Word, the church is in a unique position to articulate **what** is wrong, and **why** it is wrong. This involves the holding up of biblical standards of justice and righteousness as against the merely expedient or conventional.

For a long time, for instance, slavery was thought to be part of the nature of things, until Christian people took seriously the principle of equality in Christ. An American novelist tells the story of how for fifty years a Quaker woman was the biggest bore in all of New England: each Sunday she stood up in church and said, 'Slavery is wrong,' a tradition that dates back to all the prophets who said 'Thus saith the Lord' and brought a word of judgment against oppression.

The prophetic word is often an unwelcome intrusion, a message of doom, as with Jeremiah who for thirty years warned of the impending destruction of Jerusalem and exile to Babylon in the face of overwhelming popular consensus that God was on the side of the temple and the Jews and would not raze their religious and social order to the ground. Elijah warning Ahab of impending drought because of his apostasy, or Nathan rebuking David for his adultery, or Jesus arguing with the Pharisees over what constitutes the Law, are images of what it means to challenge the powers-that-be prophetically.

In our context it may mean speaking out against corruption and indifference to social justice on the part of the elite and the government, the insistence on due democratic process before those who would seek power by force of arms, and educating the people into a religion deeper than cultic exercises and practising justice and righteousness. The Filipino church likewise needs to turn the Word against itself in its failure to preach a gospel that liberates the poor and nurtures a people whose commitment to integrity and justice is such that our advertised reputation as being the 'only Christian nation in the Far East' is not met with a sneer and does not embarrass the cause of Christ.

The prophetic task is inclusive. It makes no difference whether one is addressing specifically moral issues like abortion or pornography, or social issues such as human rights, right-wing coups or the poor's right to survival in a heartless market economy. Scripture makes no sharp distinction between the two, as do evangelicals and the theological liberals who tend to do only one or the other. Both are legitimately part of the church's agenda: Israel was sent into exile because of **idolatry** (often pictured as 'harlotry') and **oppression**, prohetic themes resulting from the violation of the laws of love for God and one's neighbour.

Our commitment to bringing the Word of God into the political arena should not mean, however, the politicization of our reading of scripture. It is alarming how conservative elements of the Filipino church are echoing Western Christians who hotly defend capitalism as being sanctioned by the seventh commandment, Proverbs and the parable of the talents. Biblical themes of enterprise, protection of private property and prosperity as a sign of God's blessing are surfaced as arguments for the cogency of capitalism. Likewise,

Christians with socialist inclinations tend to baptize socialism as the more biblical, drawing on such concepts as stewardship rather than ownership of the earth, communal sharing of wealth and property in Acts, principles of redistribution such as the Jubilee and other legislation structuring protection for the poor.

In general, it is perhaps sufficient to infer from scripture that governments should not leave the welfare of the poor to the mysterious mechanisms of market forces that ostensibly work for the common good. In a Third-World setting where economic relations are sharply skewed and the relative strength of forces contending for scarce goods is grossly asymmetrical, it is a crime to leave the plight of the poor to the devices of those who chance their welfare to blind market forces. The detail with which scripture lays down structural legislation for the poor and the weak argues against a *laissez faire* approach to the problem of massive inequality and destitution.

At the same time, there is room for scepticism of any social system that stifles growth and individual initiative. The biblical mandate to be fruitful and multiply requires that along with distributive justice, there must be a concern that the forces that fuel an economy are optimized and given full support. We do not subscribe to a government that is no more than a welfare state, reducing labour to apathy and its people to a state of debilitation and dependency. What we need is a government whose economic policies stand decisively on the side of the poor, correcting distortions and imbalances in the system in such a way that the stage is set for both big business and small entrepreneurs to really get going, creating jobs and restoring a measure of opportunity and dignity to labour which is the only thing that is really in the hands of the poor. Governments should set the stage and manage the fiscal and social environment in such a way that economic forces are released towards the empowering of the poor to help themselves.

The collapse of socialism and the re-ordering of the world into a Pax Capitalista where growth rather than justice issues occupy center stage should caution us against tying Scripture to paradigms and ideologies that in the course of time become obsolete or are merely justifications for a heartless status quo.

The Word as both transcendent and prophetic means that it cannot be held captive to any ideological system. It is both an affirmation and a critique of whatever social system is in place. Its transforming vision, when creatively proclaimed not only by theologians and other specialists but by artists, social scientists and the like, comes as a blast of fresh air from the outside to those trapped by windowless ideologies and unimaginative social mechanics. Its biting sense of the tragic in human nature warns us of the utopian enthusiasms and disproportionate expectations of our revolutionary projects. Its hope in a kingdom that is strong even when it wears the face of weakness enables us to live with failed experiments and dreams deferred. The suffering and the glory of the cross, when kept at the center of the historical process, is both a critical and an affirming element in our fragile and doubtful battle against apparently invincible powers.

THE PRIESTLY OFFICE
Bringing the need of the world to God and the power of God to the world.

Often neglected in discussions of the social role of the church, the priestly office consists of mediating between the utter destitution of the world and the immense resources of God. It is in intercession that the church truly becomes an alternative power center, a place where social wounds can be healed and the disillusioning process of social transformation empowered by supernatural hope. It is naive to think that we can confront entrenched powers of evil with merely sophisticated techniques of political persuasion and ideological warfare. Many activist movements have been smashed not only by the iron hardness of intransigent power, but by internal collapse of will brought about by divisive dissensions and blurring of vision. Without the critiquing and empowering presence of God in the heart of our social projects, we lose our centre and purpose. Prayer is not a pious instrument by which we move God to baptise our enterprises; it is entering the strength of him who moves history and binds the powers that be.

The many casualties of political turmoil in our time need the comfort that only God through the church can give. There is need to know how exactly to bring to God the needs of refugee families displaced by war, the degradation of our poor in the cities, the problem of instability and insurgency and the demands of ethnic equality and distributive justice. Our prayer agenda must be informed, as with the prayer of Daniel (Daniel 9), lest we pray, out of political ignorance, against forces we ought to be affirming and vice versa. So many of the prayers offered by evangelicals for this nation, unfortunately, tend to veer towards the agenda of the political right.

The priestly office requires an intimacy with God that connects us with Jesus' suffering and the pain of the world and at the same time renews us with His risen life (Philippians 3:10-11). The shadow of the cross reminds us of the savage nature of evil, of how it cripples and maims human life and lurks as a hidden menace even in the good things we do. The risen Lord shields our inner spirit from assaults of despair in the face of death and other forces that break us within and convince us of defeat.

Ultimately, genuine social transformation happens in our deepest places, that part where God alone can go. Again and again, we need to remind ourselves that while the provision of services and structural mechanisms against injustice are important, social change is primarily what happens to people, in that level of being where the Spirit alone has access.

Unless prayer is somehow integrated with the warp and woof of our social activism, we are not going to reach people in that place where the conflict with evil is decisively waged.

[handwritten margin note: INSIDE → OUT APPROACH, BUT AT THE SYSTEMIC LEVEL]

THE KINGLY OFFICE
Managing the world under God

The church as reigning with the risen Jesus (Revelation 20:4, 22:5), has been understood historically as the church ruling the world in a kind of Pax Christiana, as in the Middle Ages when it rivalled state power. An alternative reading would be to see its rule as servanthood, with the church exercising dominion under the authority and power of the Suffering Servant.

To 'reign' in this sense does not mean, primarily, the holding of positions of power, but the creative subjugation of runaway forces in the world. It is a capacity for mastery given at the beginning of creation (Genesis 1:28) but somehow lost and sidetracked after the Fall (Genesis 3:16-19) and now restored to us in Jesus.

Within the economy of the kingdom, dominion is cast in terms of servanthood: 'The kings of the Gentiles exercise lordship over them ...But not so with you; rather let the greatest among you become as the youngest, and the leader as one who serves' (Luke 22:25-26).

The church is servant to society, 'hewers of wood and drawers of water,' harnessing wind and wood and water into technologies that make the world a little more habitable, or singing with the rest of creation the wonder of existence, or working side by side with all people of goodwill towards a better social order. If the church is to lead at all, it is in serving; in applying the creative energies released in Christ towards the stewardship of creation and the bringing of fallen structures closer to God's original purposes. It does not require that the church function as a worldly power, only as Daniel and Joseph who served God and their people even under alien empires.

If Christians took seriously the mandate to cultivate the earth and to rule over recalcitrant forces that seek to destroy God's world, we are less likely to suffer the severity of things such as an ecological crisis, a 'soft state' soggy with corruption, slop and sloth, monstrous traffic, mountains of refuse dumps, broken telephones, transport problems, power cuts and other ills arising not only from injustice but a mismanaged and disordered society.

Those in the Third World can rant and rail at the West for imposing inappropriate technologies in the process of competitive modernization. But unless we learn to manage faithfully our resources and develop our own technologies we shall keep being at the receiving end of industrial junk like defective nuclear power plants.

Part of the tragic nature of the Fall is that we find ourselves at the mercy of wildly savage forces of nature and runaway technologies that begin to organize and dominate human life. We have only to think of the devastating fury of Mt. Pinatubo, or the anomie and inhumanity of highly mechanized societies or the destruction of people's ways of life by the unthinking and mechanical application of developmental technologies, to realize the need to take care of the ecosystem in such a way that it works for us rather than against us, and to see to it that our technologies remain subject to us and do not develop a logic of their own, riding roughshod over the demands of community and humanness.

Concretely, this calls for Christians gifted with technical inventiveness to harness ingenuity in increasing food production, developing technologies that maximize the use of resources while maintaining sustainability and the integrity of society. It means confronting the problem of scarcity, or breakdowns in the distribution of resources, and making our social systems deliver basic services competently and efficiently. There is need to turn away from our overheated political climate and simply apply all our energies and talents to economics and making things work for our people.

POLITICS TRANSFORMS WHEN
PPL ARE " TO CHRISTIAN
IDEOLOGY ⟹ THE SYSTEM
FURTHER
ITSELF NEEDS TO BE CHRISTIAN&
BC INDIVIDUALS CANNOT DO IT.

Some concluding remarks
INVOLVEMENT AND IDENTITY

The tension intrinsic in the Church being *in* but not *of* the world has tended to polarise concern towards either **involvement** or **identity**. Faithfulness demands that we learn to live with this tension, standing in solidarity yet maintaining critical distance, immersed in our socio-historical context yet radically suspicious of our own ideological and historical conditioning.

Too often the church is reduced to mumbling in corners, occupied with its own survival and the protection of its own freedom to preach the gospel. Like the ten spies who felt unmanned by the fortified cities of Canaan, "we seem to ourselves as grasshoppers" (Numbers 13:33), too small to take on mighty powers of injustice and make a difference in the larger society. Yet history tells us that it is in times of powerlessness that the church has been most strong.

The recovery of the ancient consciousness of the demonic in power structures, and the poor as focus of compassion and liberation, warns us against undue acquiescence to the powers-that-be in a society that does not take into account the deprivation of our people. Revelation 13 should temper our enthusiasm over government in Romans 13, and the story of the rich man and Lazarus in Luke 16 should warn against a lifestyle which, while not actively exploitative, is callous towards the reality of the poor sitting at the gate.

The church as prophet, priest and king requires the gifts and resources of the whole body of Christ. Speaking the Word in places of injustice and suffering needs gifts of communicative power. Bringing a world of need to God calls for men and women who will take time to listen to God and the heart-cry of a turbulent world. Managing a bruised creation exacts costly servanthood from those whose skills and training normally go to the highest bidder in the market-place or are exported to countries of affluence. We have no right to criticise the government under which we live if we are not prepared to lay down careers for the sake of Christ and the poor.

Ultimately, forms of social involvement depend on context and the particularity of vision entrusted to each of us. It is not an accident that scripture merely outlines principles of justice and expectations out of the social order. The precise forms of governance and mechanisms by which its vision of justice and peace may be incarnated are left to the exigencies of culture and time. It has no room for the kind of ideological captivity seen in those who seek in scripture sanctions for their preferred arrangements of reality. Nor for the sort of theoretical rigidity which eliminates from its perceptual field anything which doesn't quite fit its system.

The kingdom as **here** and **not yet here** breaks open the historical process, creates new possibilities, dares us to look again in the most surprising places to find the way out of monolithic injustice. Ideological and theological fixations tend to make us miss our historical cues, unable to read the signs of the times as with the Jews of Jesus' time who kept looking elsewhere for the kingdom that had already come in their midst.

Whether our vision compels us to form communities of the King which demonstrate by power of example an alternative reality, or engage in the political process to work for social reordering, the need of the world is such that there is room for all kinds of involvement. A journalist once asked Mother Teresa why she was merely responding to outward poverty instead of rooting out its 'real source,' which was structural inequities between the rich and the poor. She replied, "That is a good idea. Why don't you do it?" As it was, she already had her hands full tending the sick and the sorrowing and the dying. Her wry answer is a backhanded challenge to those who have a different vision to work and be faithful to their own.

FOLLOW INDIVIDUAL CALLINGS
NO WORK TOWARD JUST
TRANSFORMATION IS SUPERFLUOUS

PART THREE

Kingdomkeeping:
struggles, strategies, disciplines

*S*OCIAL INVOLVEMENT is a long and often lonely task that requires a wealth of spiritual resources if it is to remain vibrant and if it is to truly tap into the transforming powers of the kingdom.

In this section, we move to a more personal narrative of lessons learned as pilgrims on our way to justice. Together we hope to journey into the ways of the cross as a controlling element in the work of social transformation. We will pay some attention to the tension between effectiveness and faithfulness, to the problem of acting decisively yet faithfully in a world that demands comformity to its own image and limits our actions to tragic choices. We shall spend some time reflecting on basic themes of our faith as buttresses for the spirit as we war against disillusionment and the loss of hope.

We conclude by anticipating the reality of the age to come as we serve the King in our time.

X
SOCIAL TRANSFORMATION
& THE DISCIPLINE OF THE CROSS

The year was 1986. Snap presidential elections had just been held in the Philippines, and the canvassing of electoral returns was going on at Batasan. Since it was becoming obvious that the then COMELEC did not know how to count, or at least counted only the votes that would perpetuate the Marcos regime, we at ISACC, together with the NAMFREL volunteers who manned with us our assigned voting precincts on election day marched to the Batasan to register protest. It seemed to us by then that the ruling power no longer had the right to rule; it was time to resist, to wave our flag, to publicly identify with all the forces that sought to unseat the strongman.

It was a very tense week. Ramos and Enrile, pillars of the regime's armed support, had not yet defected, and the 'people power' revolution, which turned the tide of battle against the Marcoses, had yet to happen. There was a calm that held the threat of menace, like the silent massing of armies in a fighting lull, a stillness that felt like the eye of a storm. Feeling that we had somehow crossed the line of no return, I took a couple of days off to go up to Baguio and pray and think about what we were doing and wherever it was the Lord was leading us. Up in the cool mountains I was suddenly seized by a fear. It occurred to me, quite belatedly, that we were but a small band of people who could get wiped out along with the rest if the monstrous might of state power turned its guns on the protesters — a clamp-down that did not seem unlikely at the time. Was I taking unnecessary risks? Was it irresponsible to show our hand so publicly like that? (Our people and our placards and streamers were photographed and splashed in the pages of Newsweek and Asiaweek and local magazines existing at the time.) We were but a small group of people who had yet to disciple others who will come after us. What would happen to the institution, to the vision that would die with us?

For once, I understood why heads of institutions tend to be conservative. It is the job of the leader to fight for the institution, to minimize risks and see to it that it survives in the face of pressure to act precipitately in a crisis. I was my usual headstrong self in taking the risks and initiatives that we had taken. But up in the mountains, I saw with a hard clarity what we were up against. I felt fear. It was then that these words of Jesus came back to me: 'unless a grain of wheat falls to the ground and dies, it remains alone; but if it dies, it bears much fruit...' (John 12:24)

The words had stayed with me since then, reeling in my brain and rolling in the depths of my soul. They came echoing in those moments in the barricades when we were face to face with charging tanks and soldiers in battle gear and I could feel the warm press of bodies throbbing and quivering in fear and excitement. The words welled up inside me that fateful dawn when I hugged my little sister and sent her home and prayed with friends and colleagues who gathered around me as we hugged and said goodbye to each other, thinking that the break of day would be our last as news of oncoming troops blared from the radio and we could hear the rumble of tanks coming down Ortigas Avenue. They came humming in my brain that one fine morning when the crowd had thinned out and we were left like ragtag stragglers at the gate of Camp Crame to make what looked like a hopeless, desperate, and quixotic stand against the oncoming assault of helicopter gunships buzzing overhead.

Those words of Jesus had assumed a mythic proportion within me, dense with meanings that I could feel but could not articulate. I knew that at the centre of them was the sense that discipleship is a dance of death, and the assurance that within the economy of the kingdom, dying is always productive. But always it seemed to be saying something more...

The words were spoken at that stage when Gentiles from far off were feeling the pull of who Jesus was, and Jesus, increasingly weighed by the prospect of his passion, declares that the hour had come for him to be glorified (John 12:20-23). Intuitively, Jesus seemed to connect the widening of the gospel's frontier to the prospect of his dying: 'unless the grain of wheat falls... it remains alone.' Solidarity with others is premised on a death somewhere within us.

The second part of the sentence links this kind of dying to being productive: 'but if it dies, it bears much fruit.' Dying is the straight and narrow road to seeing the work of our hands multiply tenfold.

These two principles, dying as a condition for solidarity, and dying as a way to fertility, are seen concretely in the career of Jesus. To be a man for others, Jesus, says Paul, "emptied" himself and became obedient unto death (Philipians 2:7,8). The trappings of deity were not "a thing to be grasped," instead, Jesus divested himself of all that belonged to his previous status and took the form of a servant (Philippians 2:6-7). He did not stop there; the process of his humiliation was to end in death.

But precisely because of his acceptance of suffering, God has highly exalted him and bestowed on him a name which is above every name; his territorial reach expands to include not only those in heaven but those on earth and under the earth, and we are told that in the face of rebellion and blasphemy every knee shall bow and every conceivable tongue shall confess that Jesus is Lord (Philippians 2:9-11).

What does this mean to those of us who are engaged in social transformation?

First, it seems to me that we cannot have an incarnation without experiencing some form of crucifixion. To be involved, to be immersed in solidarity with others, is to be vulnerable in those places where we are by nature or by social circumstance strong.

Kenosis or 'self-emptying' in our case may mean laying down careers and the benefits of an education — stepping down from being development experts to being listeners and fellow learners in a community. It may mean surrendering the right to be comfortable, to taking with us the baggage of our culture or class, and taking on the standards of the culture and the style of life of the people we serve. "To the Jew I became a Jew... To the weak I became weak," says Paul (1 Corinthians 9:20-22). It is this accommodative power, this readiness for self-effacement, which controls what we mean by identification. The process involves not merely an agile facility for adaptation, the sort of 'bamboo dancing' Filipinos are so good at doing in a clash of cultures, but the willingness to humble ourselves in a way that hurts. Jesus was not simply prepared to fast and pray and go to the synagogue and eat kosher food like any good Jew; he 'made himself nothing' in such a way that his own people snorted at suggestions that he could be the Messiah: "Isn't he the carpenter's son?" said the folk back home at Nazareth (Matthew 13:55). He had so rooted himself among them that his townmates thought they knew exactly who he was and where he had come from.

Second, 'obedience unto death' is the only way to genuine fruit-fulness and spiritual power in our work.

In Jesus' brief career there were many temptations to distract him away from the cross. The first occasion was right after his baptism, when, full of the Holy Spirit, he was driven into the wilderness and subjected to severe testing. The experience of power from on high must have given him other ideas of what he could do for his people: turn stones into bread like an economic reformer, perform signs and wonders as a miracle worker or engage in strongman politics like the autocratic but revered Caesar (Matthew 4:1-11, Luke 4:1-13).

In the same way, those of us who wish to serve the poor are under constant pressure to reduce the work of social transformation to a matter of mere economics or strong political will or even a spectacular show of spiritual power. All these things are, of course, important — Jesus did feed the poor by performing economic miracles. He was sufficiently independent of political authority to be perceived as a threat to both the religious and political establishment. He healed the sick and performed many signs and wonders for the benefit of incredulous Jews who looked for signs. But from the very start of his public career, he understood that his was a calling deeper than any of these. It was no less than the wresting of the entire world order from the strongholds of evil: "Now is the judgment of this world, now shall the ruler of this world be cast out..." (John 12:31). Quite strangely, this overthrowing of the 'prince of the power of the air' did not happen by the use of force nor by populist programmes such as feeding the poor and entertaining them with the psychic highs of a spiritual circus. The powers were defeated, not by a show of force, but by the nailing of the Son of God on a cross, a shedding of blood that mysteriously effected forgiveness and the disarming of principalities and powers (Hebrews 9:22, Colossians 2:13-15).

While the sacrificial work of Christ is unique, there is something about the willingness to suffer pain and loss for the sake of integrity and higher goals that brings forth a deeper impact and effectiveness. This is what I learned in those fateful days of momentous events in the history of the Filipino people. We could have made our calculations, and hung on to the survival of our institution as a primary consideration in our actions. We could have waited willy-nilly, as some did, to see where the wind was blowing before we made our move. We could have played it safe, and thereby missed our historical cues by failing to respond decisively to a *kairos* moment in our history. Thankfully, instinct told us that solidarity or the doing of justice take precedence over self-preservation. Like Abraham who offered up Isaac, I figured that in some mysterious way our ranks will get resurrected in some other form — I only wished we were there to see it. I am not privy to what was going on inside the million or so other people who converged at EDSA to make their bodies count against the dictatorship. It is possible that like me, every one made a choice in that part of us which now and again shines with a purer, clearer flame and leaves us in no doubt as to the rightness of the choices we make. Without much calculation, our people rose to the call of the hour, and God honored the faith that gave us courage to stand for things higher and larger than ourselves. In spite of the thwarting of its promise, what we did at EDSA resonated among freedom-loving peoples of the world. I suspect that much of the reason had to do with this same promise of fruitfulness to any gesture of loyalty to the ways of him who overrules history.

Third, the work of Christ on the cross reminds us that social action is a confrontation with the powers-that-be. We are, ultimately, not battling against flesh and blood nor merely dismantling unjust social systems; we are confronting the powers in their cosmic and social dimensions.

In any work of deep social transformation, we need to ask: **who** or **what** demonic powers are entrenched in our social system? Is it Mammon? Is it the spirit of injustice, the spirit of indiscipline and futility? Is it those subhuman forces that go by such names as 'Kamag-anak Inc.,' 'colonialism,' 'market dominance,' 'multinational,' 'debt'? What about the undue concentration of interest in apparitions, healing miracles, dancing suns and Santo Niños, and other forms of spiritual spectacles? Are we truly able to articulate the meaning of the demonic in the Philippines or are we merely fighting shadows, misled by the thousand guises under which evil hides its sinister plots and deodorizes its muck?

Apart from **naming** the powers, we need to see to it that a **transfer of power** has actually taken place. Has Jesus' lordship become a social fact or has it remained a powerless confession? As in a genuine conversion, is our work of transformation moving people from the worship of society's idols to allegiance to what Jesus represents? Are the people we serve becoming people of the kingdom and not merely middle class Filipinos whose aspirations go no higher than the glitzy fantasies of going Stateside and pursuing the American Dream?

Finally, the cross is an invitation to take part in the "fellowship of his suffering." (Philippians 3:10). There is no room here for triumphalism, for the sort of blithe can-do mentality which naively thinks it will change the world by sheer effort and enthusiasm. Evil is so strong that it sent the very Son of God to the cross. Similarly, those who seek to confront the powers that be are likely to experience the full force of the enemy. We must understand that in standing against evil in its social and structural expressions we are putting ourselves at the center of demonic opposition.

It is not an accident that people engaged in social transformation suffer tremendous opposition and even persecution; battle-scarred, the psychological wounds go so deep that some go through their life and work forever handicapped by the ever recurring memory of pain. Often, all that the devil has to do to neutralize the work is to make the people in it so tired they burn out into uselessness and become sidetracked. Colleagues in non-governmental organizations tell me that in two years their people in the field burn out and need to get pulled out. Much of the 'compassion fatigue' that afflicts social activists perhaps has its roots in the inability to discern the difference between dedication and drivenness. Those motivated by the former are ever conscious of who it is we serve; those who are propelled by the latter are hardly conscious of the blind impulses behind their monomaniac zealousness. It is important to locate the source of our energy and find the well-springs of sustenance and hope: where does the power come from? What forces rule our lives? What keeps us going through years and years of battering doors of injustice and deprivation?

The unflinching recognition that the work of transformation will drag us to the cross finds its solace in the fact that this is not the end of the story. We shall rise again, and from the forces of darkness and defeat wrest a deeper knowing of the power of Jesus and his resurrection life (Philippians 3:10). Christ has been given a name above every other name; before this name every power on earth and under the earth is forced to bow the knee, no matter how reluctantly.

Our forebears, perhaps, would know the full force of what this means. My grandfather warded off evil spirits and healed sickness by the appropriate use of the prescribed **dasal** or **oracion**. Like many others in this culture, he was acquainted with the spirit world and knew the power of invocation, of calling on the names of higher powers for protection against forces of ill-will and ill-health. While it is possible that some of the prayers and magic words may have been the names of demonic powers higher in the hierarchy of principalities, there was at least the sense that one could appeal to a higher spirit, a higher name, and find genuine relief from disease and the spell of evil fortune. In the same vein, Paul tells us the tremendous news that because Jesus was obedient unto death, God has highly exalted him, giving him a name above every other name in all the worlds conceivable to us. His is a principality without boundaries, and his name can compel the most powerful and recalcitrant forces to do as we have asked. To invoke this name in the work of transformation is to summon the immense and unparalleled resources of God to defeat the powers that oppress human life.

In times and cultures where the church is ascendant, it is easy for the people of God to take ethical shortcuts and rely on newfound political power, with feeding miracles or supernatural signs of power as primary ways of responding to the problem of the poor. Experience shows that these are not enough. We need to engage the powers at that level where they are truly disarmed, and this means acceptance of humiliation, obedience unto death and confidence in the risen and exalted Christ.

XI
SURVIVAL STRATEGIES
Developing a Sense of the Possible

The great Italian statesman Camilo Cavour was once asked what he thought was the most essential trait needed by a statesman. He replied, "a sense of the possible." I submit that this faculty is needed just as much by people engaged in social transformation as by politicians. The ability to calibrate expectations to discern what could be pushed to the limits of the possible and what is best left to a more opportune time and circumstance, is a critical element in furthering the cause of the kingdom. We need to be able to make strategic choices, advancing the possible good even as we seek the impossible best.

In the rough-and-tumble world of politics we are confronted with the problem of mediating between a hard pragmatism and futile idealism, between what is possible and what is principled. The tragic nature of bringing about change in a fallen world grabs us by the collar and brings us face to face with the difficulty of maintaining consistency between ends and means, of the struggle to find a way of coming to terms with rough realism without surrender of idealism.

How can we be effective in a world that thwarts our best intentions? How do we make significant contribution in a society that marginalizes its best and most creative people and yet is disillusioned by its own aberrations? The answers to these questions are complex and deserve more lengthy treatment. For the moment, it is perhaps sufficient to arm ourselves with some survival skills that would enable us and our ideals to withstand the test of realism. The following are some survival strategies I have found helpful.

1. Expect a self-developed opposition
Mao Tse Tung, the late great patron saint of socialists, once said that the process of change moves 'two steps forward, one step backward.' A nation or a cause that takes a giant leap forward usually suffers a backlash from forces threatened or displaced by the great effort. A movement develops an antithesis, a reaction that sets it back, but the

resulting synthesis from the conflict is at least one degree higher in quality than where things were before.

The parable of the wheat and the weeds (Matthew 13:24-30) antedates this dialectical understanding of the process of change. We are told that for every advance in the kingdom of God, there is a corresponding advance in the kingdom of darkness. When the wheat shot up and bore grain, the weeds appeared also.

It is not surprising that the seeds of opposition and contradiction are usually seen within, and not outside, the forces of change. The demonic is by nature unimaginative; it can only imitate, and destroys by imitating the good work of God. Much hurt and damage is caused, not by enemies without, but by enemies within. This is what normally breaks up churches and movements. One can handle severe opposition from the world without, but not the hearthbreak of bitter conflict and betrayal in the hands of one's own people.

Yet the Master tells us that we just have to learn to live so closely with the dark side of the work we do. "Let both grow together until the harvest," he tells us; the two kingdoms are so inextricably linked, it is not possible to uproot one without uprooting the other. We just have to be prepared to consolidate our gains in the face of internal dissension and the constant raising of contradictions, fighting off the erosion of the good that has been done by the steadfast application of grit and grace.

Scripture is clear that upsetting the existing order is dangerous business. "He who digs a pit will fall into it," says the Teacher, "a serpent will bite him who breaks through a wall" (Ecclesiastes 10:8). Taking action and initiative entails a lot of risk, and is liable to get us into trouble. Wisdom means that we learn to take calculated risks, knowing exactly what it will cost us to pioneer new ways of doing things.

2. Inspire and nurture a strategic minority

Students of social change tell us that it is better to aim at consensus within a strategic minority rather than to waste time and breath at soliciting the conformity of the majority.

Since a movement for change involves vision and sacrifice it is not possible to start with the many. Very few people can see ten steps ahead of them. Most are enclosed in the realities of the present to be able to imagine an alternative future. It takes a lot of imagination to believe that with the coming of Christ, a new order has come into being. There is a new world out there, waiting to come to historical fruition for men and women of faith and vision who dare to believe that things can be other than they are.

Also, it is painful and hard work to invest in a movement in its infancy. People subject causes, like any other involvement, to a cost-benefit analysis. Since, in its incipient stage there is hardly any return, either in the form of psychological reward or visible success, a cause to begin moving needs John-the-Baptist types who are prepared to be lonely voices in the wilderness, able to subsist on rudimentary fare such as locusts and wild honey for the sake of a vision burning in their eyes.

This strategic minority needs to be nurtured into what sociologists call a 'critical mass': people of vision and sacrifice who in turn are able to influence a great number of people around them. Development strategists call them 'multipliers,' and they are not necesssarily those who occupy top positions in organizations or communities. They are usually natural leaders, with personality and functional gifts that draw people around them, a fact that sometimes threatens formal authorities or established leadership.

While this minority is capable of great endurance to begin with they nevertheless need a great deal of cognitive support, a sense that they stand in the mainstream of the movement of God in history, even if in their time they are pushed to the sidelines and marginalized. They need to feel part of a great tradition, "surrounded by so great a cloud of witnesses" as the writer to the Hebrews puts it (Hebrews 12:1). To support them, we need to articulate this continuity, this sense of being part of a long line of witnesses, like the prophets in Israel of old who were killed and stoned by their own people.

Besides cognitive support, nurturance of this significant minority requires personal discipling, the sort of intimacy the disciples enjoyed in the life of Jesus. Movements develop because of a deep personal and relational pull at their centre. People, ultimately, do not relate to the abstract ideals of institutions; they relate to people, to the quality of leadership behind them. In a time when even church leaders have become as inaccessible as political big shots, with a cordon sanitaire that makes people feel they are approaching the presence of someone very nearly like God, we need to recover a capacity for intimacy with our own people. We need to take time for people who are perhaps as ordinary as the fishermen Peter and James and John, but nevertheless have fire within them and the potential for turning the world upside down. Without this intimate shepherding interest in our people, we may become efficient managers of development organizations or successful executives of church institutions, but not leaders of movements whose ideals resonate within a larger and larger circle of what Tolkien once called 'the fellowship of the Ring' — a humanly vulnerable yet tight solidarity of people who are deeply attached to one another, drawing warmth and sustenance from the fierce fire of commitment and love that is at the centre of what binds them together.

Sociologists tell us that it takes only five percent of a country's population to turn society around and put it on course. Social renewal begins when a strategic minority hears the call of a new order, catches a vision of what is possible and gives their all to the birth of a coming world.

3. Watch your wineskins

A student of church movements once said that sociologically, a community of people with a cause moves from being a movement to a machine, and from machine to a monument. The early stage where a movement generates excitement because its ideas are fresh, its leadership charismatic, and its mission sharp and clear, soon gives way to a stage where things get more efficient because routinized: charisma is ritualized, purpose becomes platform, and conviction is systematized into a creed. If this continues and no fresh element reforms or reshapes the institution, it hardens and petrifies into a monument, a sad relic of the days gone by when the Spirit blew and blasted to bits sacrosanct ways of doing things.

For a movement to retain its cutting edge, it is important to hold nothing sacred except its original calling. Institutions, programs and structures are only means; we must be ready to discard them once they have outlived their usefulness. As a wise old man once said to me, "You should never be afraid to let anything die."

The media prophet Mcluhan, sensing quick obsolescence in the face of rapid advances in technology and material culture, once said that "if it works, it's obsolete". He means that once we have perfected a way of doing things it cannot be improved upon and is therefore on its way to becoming obsolete.

Mcluhan's remark is really only a modern restatement of Jesus' saying about wine and wineskins (Luke 5:37-39). Like Judaism, wineskins are going to age; in contrast, the new wine of the gospel is always new, bursting old wineskins that can no longer contain the force of its dynamic. Church structures, like fasting and sabbath rules and other institutions of Jesus' time, are always on the way to becoming obsolete. They may have served us well in the past, like the cherished Old English words of a sixteenth-century prayer book or an old hymn that stirs memories of the religion of one's childhood or of the hardier, more uncompromising faith of our forebears. But like the way of all flesh, good things die or ought to be retired.

Like church structures, a movement's programs and strategies need to change as objective social conditions change. Much of the marginalization and perceived obsolescence of the hard Left, for instance, has to do with the inability to read changing historical cues. As people of the kingdom, we need to be able to always hear the changing context of our people along with the timeless imperatives of our text if we are to discern the movement of the Spirit in our time.

Besides the constant pressure of relevance, we also need to factor in the element of the demonic as the movement develops into a more organized institution. It is not an accident that our institutions tend to run away from us, developing distortions that are the exact opposite of the ideals they are supposed to serve. Without vigilant control, they soon grow into unwieldy monsters, a recalcitrance that resists prophetic critique, bidding us serve their own ends rather than the purpose for which they were established in the first place. Self-perpetuation of the system begins to override the original aims, something we see in many churches and non-governmental organizations which end up fighting, not for the vitality of the cause they serve, but for the survival of their institutions in the name of such catch words as 'orthodoxy,' 'efficiency,' or 'sustainability.'

In the same way that Sabbath regulations, for instance, were distorted into tools for oppression rather than instruments of liberation and comfort from the pressing drudgery of human work, our institutions can became idols that bid us serve **them** rather than serve **us** or the ideals we mean to serve by having them. Lest they run away from us, concious effort must be expended in seeing to it that our structures remain leashed to our original purposes. There is a rebelliousness intrinsic to structures that have managed to organize into systems or a self-sustaining force. This thrusting towards heedless autonomy is a mark of the demonic that needs to be carefully watched and subdued. Let us take care that our institutions do not develop a logic of their own, establishing a hegemony that is not only independent but destructive of the reforming impulse that gave birth to them, sometimes even crushing some of the most creative individuals within or marginalizing and expelling them.

In this case, not only is the wineskin confused for the wine, but the new wine itself is refused. As Jesus warns, "no one after drinking old wine desires new; for he says, 'the old is good'" (Luke 5:39). We can get so used to the taste of the old that when the new wine comes we tend to spit it out.

4. Play the Pied Piper

Truly creative movements do not need huge organizations to carry out what they need to do. What is crucial is the ability to discern what God is doing in the world, and articulate it at certain critical junctures.

This is what I learned in those critical days at EDSA. At dawn Sunday morning we decided to risk adding ourselves to the body-count and rally those of our people who wish to do the same. We stationed ourselves at Gate Two of Camp Aguinaldo and issued an announcement through Radio Veritas and DZAS.

With adrenalin running high, I rattled off strategies of how to mobilize evangelical people together. The mood was upbeat, excitement was high, and we all felt the fire that descends upon us when we know in our bones that we have been inspired. Then in the heat and flurry of preparations, someone interjected an observation that stopped us in our tracks: "Who are we anyway to mobilize the evangelicals?" There was a pause. I thought of the soldiers trapped like rats within the walls of the camp, and how it was so right simply to be there, even if we represented but a small minority of evangelical Christians. "Never mind," I said. "Let us issue a call, and let him who hears hear it."

The turnout was amazing. Churches from faraway places came, whole busloads from Bulacan, Batangas, Tagaytay and other nearby provinces. We had always thought that we had a following among more thoughtful and sophisticated churches, those with fairly large contingents of professionals who, like us, trace their roots to Inter-Varsity or other student movements. Quite predictably, they all came. But it was a surprise to me to see so many other grassroots churches, simple folk who had come because they heard a call within them and knew it was right to come and be counted. As a mother cuddling a child said to me, "We just want to be here. *Gusto naming makiisa. May ginagawa ang Panginoon dito. Nararamdaman lang namin na pinapunta niya kami rito.*" The vast masses of the people who gathered at EDSA had no theology nor ideology behind what they felt they needed to do. It was enough that they heard a call somewhere in the depths of themselves, something deeper, higher and larger, something to do with justice and freedom and other things they knew by instinct to be somehow related to God.

It is not necessarily a weakness that the events at EDSA lacked conscious theological or revolutionary premises. The mass of men and women do not need closely reasoned arguments in order to act. It is perhaps sufficient that a few should discern and articulate the moral imperatives of a critical time. Often, all that is needed is for someone to bravely raise a flag, to say 'here we stand; we can do no other,' and then everyone comes out of the woodwork, silent no more and unwillling to stand injustice any longer.

There are, of course, few causes as universal as the one fought for at EDSA, something big enough to resonate within large masses

87

of people. It is a rare moment in history when forces on the side of the good and the bad are so very clearly drawn. Still, experience shows that at critical junctures, there ought to be those who are alert enough to perceive a *kairos* moment, able to hear the thud of God's footfall when it comes as an accent to human history, articulating it for the vast masses of people who for the most part can feel it coming in the air but have no words for it.

To play the Pied Piper, to sing a tune that our people will recognize as their own, echoing their own longings and aspirations — this is the job of those of us who wish to see society transformed. "My sheep hear my voice," says Jesus (John 10:27). In so far as we are hearing that voice when it speaks, amplifying it for all to hear and allowing it to be at the centre of our loyalties, there will always be those who will hear us, people who are given to us to nurture and care for. There will be sheep who will follow.

Part of the discipline of being in community is that we do not expect that everyone should follow us or hear that part of the voice we are hearing from God. We cannot absolutize our vision, wanting everyone to take the path of obedience that we have taken. God speaks uniquely to different parts of his church. We should allow for plurality of agendas, and even plain narrowness, while expecting widespread consensus in those rare moments when the hand of God comes down decisively and overturns history.

God, ultimately, is able to speak and mobilize his people when necessary: "The sheep hear my voice." All that we are asked to do is to hear it ourselves and sing it for our people, sing it faithfully and sing it well so that they, too, may recognize his song and thus prove to be his own.

5. Protect your inner life

There is something about the daily exposure to poverty and other ills of society which tends to wear away faith and makes agents of change some of the most cynical people around. Poverty is evil; it grinds people down and distorts the best of us into churlish whiners or wooden prophets of doom and gloom in whose eyes the light has gone dead.

The Teacher gives us a curious piece of advice: "Be not righteous overmuch, and do not make yourself overwise, why should you destroy yourself?" (Ecclesiastes 7:16). There is more than a hint here that there is a seeking after righteousness which tends to get disproportionate, — perhaps the sort that borders on fanaticism, or, in some, the passion for perfection which cannot countenance frustration. The insistence on justice, the unwavering commitment to find redress for wrong, ought to remain unsurrendered. However, this should not mean the inability to rejoice at small gains, nor the incapacity to allow for failure and setbacks. At the heart of our faith is the consciousness that our work is fragile. "All flesh is like grass, and all its glory like the flower of grass; the grass withers, and the flower falls" (Isaiah 40:6-7). We cannot ask too much. As Luther once advised, "If you cannot move a stone, let it lie." We cannot be 'overrighteous' or 'overwise', banging our heads against the wall when the struggle for justice and insight seems a losing proposition. "Why should you destroy yourself?" asks the Teacher.

A critical skill we need to teach ourselves and our people is how to fail — how to learn our lessons from the experience of defeat and pick ourselves up again and start anew. This, according to Paul, is how we endure. "We are afflicted in every way, but not crushed; perplexed, but not driven to despair; persecuted, but not forsaken; struck down, but not destroyed; always carrying in the body the death of Jesus so that the life of Jesus may also be manifested in our bodies." (2 Corinthians 4:8-10) With readiness, we carry in our bodies the marks of the cross, but also the hope and power of Jesus' risen life.

Paul tells us to "put on the whole armor of God," and makes mention of the "shield of **faith**, with which you can quench the flaming darts of the evil one" (Ephesians 6:13-17). In our constant contact with the powers of evil, there is need to insulate ourselves, to put up a shield in such a way that evil and its canker cannot penetrate nor make an assault in our inner spirit. In this we need the ability to keep faith, to hang on to a basic belief in innocence and the power of goodness.

Protecting our inner life also means that we practice a certain amount of detachment. A contemplative once said that "the best way to care for the world is not to care." Involvement and the need to see some success can easily become idols, absorbing all our energies and devouring all we hold dear. To disengage, we need periodic flights of fancy that are just as absorbing, a strategic withdrawal into an entirely different world, where the dragon is slain and the prince rescues and runs off with the maiden. Like the poor who escape drudgery by retreating into fantasy, or the prisoner who likes to talk of the smell and colour of the world outside and refuses to dwell on the humdrum dreariness of prison life, we should not fault ourselves for wanting the fresh and free air of an imagination that brings relief from the pressures of a world that would not yield to our changing.

A sanity escape, at its best, is really a longing for sabbath, for that time and space when we can rightly disengage and behold the work of our hands as something removed from us. Seven times in the creation narrative we are told that "God saw that it was good;" from time to time he would detach himself, as it were, and look over the thing that he had made, until, finally, he surveyed all that he had made — the whole, vast and intricate finish of it — and "behold, it was very good" (Genesis 1:4, 10, 12, 18, 21, 25, 31).

The sabbath is an institution created to release us from a monomaniac obsession with work, to allow us to reflect on it from a distance and cast a critical look at its actual worth and significance. Seen from the center, from the core of that which gives us ultimate meaning, our work gets relativized before the Creator and assumes its rightful proportion. Apart from the relief from stress that it affords, the sabbath delivers us from the temptation to worship the work of our hands, from an uncritical and disproportionate sense of its importance. Messianism begins when we ignore the critiquing and proportioning element that use of the Sabbath brings.

It is also important to recognize that social transformation requires a long obedience, and there are times when we suffer what Alan Sillitoe calls the 'loneliness of the long-distance runner.' Changing structures is a marathon effort of long gestation; it is not a dash or a sprint with cheerers on the sidelines. This means we consciously develop endurance, the ability to outlast the opposition and prevail in a long war of attrition.

"If you faint in the day of adversity," says scripture, "your strength is small" (Proverbs 24:10). While this may sound obvious and even facetious, it wryly reminds us of the need to increase our strength so that we have sufficient reserves for days of extreme pressure and stress. As the Lord tells the prophet Jeremiah, "If you have raced with men on foot, and it has wearied you, how will you compete with horses?" (Jeremiah 12:5).

Let us remember that we are up against a foe that in many ways is bigger, brighter, brassier, with massive resources and access to technology that enables it to replicate itself. Beside institutionalized forces of evil, forces of good are usually ragtag bands of do-gooders hardly able to get their act together. It is an unequal contest. We are not competing with mere men; we are competing with horses.

Since our strength is small, we should learn to conserve energy. Strategically, this means we get selective about our fights. We must learn to pass up small provocations to conserve gunpowder for the big battles. An ancient Chinese general once said that the best way to win a war is to try not to fight. If we can skirt a skirmish we should. If we can manage to advance our forces without firing a single shot, then let us do so. Open confrontation decimates not only the ranks of the enemy but also our own.

Conserving energy also means that we move with the timing of the seasons; we should not force things to come to a head if they have yet to come to fruition. A sense of timing is important; much useless activity can be prevented by a simple sense of where people are at any given moment. Too many movements fritter away their opportunities by getting caught up with scattered initiatives that are prematurely launched, in the process failing to muster the necessary effort for a big challenge looming ahead.

Ultimately, transforming society is really the work of God; we can neither add nor subtract to what he is already doing. If it is a time for change, it is a time for change; if it is a time for war, it is a time for war. All that we can do is to discern the hand of God when he acts in history and respond accordingly. "Consider the work of God: who can make straight what he has made crooked?" (Ecclesiastes 7:13). There is a mystery to the hard intransiegence of evil; only God, ultimately, can make it straight.

91

May God grant us the capacity to change what we can change, and leave to his sovereign love the hardness of crooked things. Because of our own great need, let us listen to him and walk with him through the perils of this long dark night as we wait and watch for the small, slow flame that signals daylight.

XII
THE PRACTICE OF RADICAL PESSIMISM
Taking Evil Seriously

Since our 'people power' revolution in the Philippines years ago, political thinking in this country has been fraught with suggestions of unappropriated initiatives, failed expectations, prostrate power and military violence, which make succeeding governments vulnerable to charges of repeating the terrors of the old order. Malaise and cynicism very quickly took hold of the Aquino government, which was the first government installed by direct people power. It failed in its own promises, and people lost confidence in the historical process which began when they brought down a Marcos regime heavy with its own extravagant contradictions.

Filipinos underwent a 'revolution of risen expectations,' for once feeling a sense of what they could actually do. Then came the test of realism, and, at once, resolve broke down before the hardness of structural injustice, and the long and arduous work of rebuilding a nation. Long ravaged, people felt the lingering distortions of a shattered political tradition, a legacy of colonialism and military interventionism, a ruined economy and the atavistic inertia of fierce survival instincts in the face of deepened poverty and brutal imbalances in society.

Once auspicious signs to a viable future progressively revealed a dark underside. The return to political normalcy signalled the collapse of the rainbow coalition and the return of traditional politics and the opportunistic use of formal democratic processes. A renegade military wing, made conscious of its political potential by a chance success at reading the right cues, arrogated to itself the task of guiding the political order by a series of coups and inept attempts to ingratiate themselves with the popular imagination. 'People power' deteriorated into distorted exercises of misguided political will by a Marcos loyalist fringe screaming in the streets or a dangerously armed cadre of vigilantes let loose in the name of faith and freedom to track down communists.

In politics, as in much of life, there is this tragic tendency to move towards a dark underside, or a self-developed contradiction — an antithesis, if you like, which taunts us like Goethe's Mephistopheles — a solemn, melancholy thorn in the side described as 'a spirit that always denies,' an annoying yet darkly seductive radical doubt that puts to constant question the best that we believe. The result for some is a creeping dissilusionment, an intemperate realism that in the end takes away the spring and lightness in our steps, stoops the shoulders and makes us bitterly huddle in corners, muttering in the dark like Plato's cavemen vegetating ineffectually on the inaccessible meaning of shadows.

Scripture has an ancient name for this: sin. By this, it makes us understand that the problems of the world have to do not merely with faulty social systems or a historical handicap like colonization but a radical infirmity that lies closer to home: the perverse state of our hearts. It is not an accident that commonsensical people equate humanness with frailty: *'sapagkat kami ay tao lamang.'* Intuitively, we all know that there is that in us which buckles down before temptations to betray our ideals, to surrender integrity and take the path of least resistance towards the softer option of security rather than the painstaking hardship of involvement and solidarity. In spite of socialization and external controls, something in us runs haywire and breaks convention, a lawlessness that in some takes the relatively harmless form of a sneering iconoclasm and in others the runaway proportions of a crime.

Sin in Scripture is more than breaking some law, be it moral or legal. It is, to Jeremiah, a darkness in the heart whose depths are fathomless: "The heart of man is desperately corrupt; who can know it?" (Jeremiah 17:9). The shock of Hitler or a ruthless dictator reveals this, but so does our silent complicity in their dark doings or the willingness of many to opt for the convenience of bribery when faced with bureaucratic knavery. That power corrupts, and absolute power corrupts absolutely, means not that power structures cause people to become warped, but that a contamination already implicit in the human condition is afforded opportunity to spread itself according to the degree of latitude allowed by the system. 'The horror, the horror!'

94

is the fated cry of those who, like Conrad's Kurtz, would set themselves up as a law unto themselves, only to discover that the dizzy heights would lead them to a vast and heartless carelessness, and the utter blackness of having intimately looked at the heart of darkness.

Total depravity was how the Reformers described it, meaning there is not a single part of us which remains uninfected by a bias in our nature towards evil. Reason, for instance, that great hope of children of the Enlightenment, degenerates into rationalization, and is often powerless to govern recalcitrant passions. As Paul puts it, "I do not understand what I do. For what I want to do, I do not do, but what I hate, I do" (Romans 7:15).

Those who know the fierceness of what it takes to struggle against personal failure will recognize that there is a 'war among the members,' a deadly conflict in our natures. Through the ages, it has found classic expression in literature's formulary dilemmas between the head and the heart, Dr. Jekyll and Mr. Hyde, the whore and the madonna, and the complex, cosmic vascillations of Hamlet the contemplative within Hamlet the prince who must act decisively to save the state from the corrosive atmosphere of royal rot.

A poet-critic once observed that there are really only two kinds of writers: those who believe in original sin, and those who do not. One either believes in the perfectibility of the human race by progressive materialist evolution, or in the tragic lostness of a fallen race continually thwarted by its own intrinsic aberrations. The distinction also seems to hold true for social analysts. One either believes that a little more social engineering would take us to a stage of common commitment to collective good or hopes at best that mechanisms could be found by which human capacity for harm and self-seeking could be limited and constrained.

That we are at best diciplined by order and tradition into something fairly decent is at the heart of Christianity's prophetic and critical refusal to be unduly impressed by party platforms. It has no great passion for the abstract symmetry of ideology or dogma nor for disproprotionate claims circulating in the marketplace about the solubility of social problems by the right application of profit incentives and technique.

Radical skepticism over the possibilities of unredeemed human nature restrains enthusiasm over social experiments and revolutionary projects. It does not believe that a little more education or a more sophisticated system of reward and punishment would turn people into persuadable citizens of Skinner's Walden II. Neither does it look forward to seeing a 'new man' emerge out of historico-economic forces, nor does it buy the notion of a fat society built out of enlightened self-interest and untrammeled enterprise. At the same time, the lack of great expectations makes it possible to remain undeterred by failure or postponement of success. "Hope deferred makes the heart sick," says the writer of Proverbs (13:12). Despair is the property of those who expect much, and have not yet learned the modulating pragmatism of a radical pessimism that rejoices at simply having endured because haunted by a constant sense of the possibility of failure. Consciousness of what the poet Auden calls 'human unsuccess,' allows acceptance of failure, openness to the untidy irregularities and incongruities of our experience, not to mention sympathy and solidarity with those whose intelligence resides in the stomach and makes them happily impervious to attempts at social management.

Belief in the basic intractability of human behavior does not mean, however, surrender to the forces of disorder and domination. It is precisely because we are pessimistic about human nature that we insist on structural limits to the destructive potential of sin in social life. If it is naive to be unduly optimistic about political programmes, it is equally simple-minded to forsake structural solutions to complex problems of distributive justice. If social change is not merely a matter of problem-solving or tinkering with the machine, it is also not merely a matter of converting individuals as Christians tend to assume. The slogan, 'more Christians means a more just society' simply does not follow; the old ruling class of South Africa was said to be mostly made up of decent, church-going people, yet apartheid remained entrenched for many years as a system of racial oppression. The much-publicized renewal of the Filipino church has yet to yield evidence of having contributed to greater justice in this country. It is wishful thinking to blithely assume that more religion and a few more sermons on love will do the job of breaking up glacial structures of injustice. "The world is full of good men," says a novelist writing on the horrors of the American Civil War, yet everyday, "the world drives hard into madness."

How then do we wrest hope out of the disappointments of our national life and the implacable nature of systemic social problems? As has been said, it helps to have a highly-developed sense of the tragic, an awareness of the sin principle as it operates in public life. Things self-destruct, and human beings being what they are, will ensure that the experiment fails and that our dreams vanish like crouching shadows before daylight. "To be a man," someone says, "is both a crime and a penance." We hurt others by being what we are and are punished by the daily failure of not being what we want to be.

At the same time, we need to be reminded again and again that the Christian story believes in happy endings. Although we are not afraid of looking in the eye the shadows that surround our own efforts at justice-seeking, we believe, ultimately, in the power of goodness, and the happy issue of whatever good it is that we do.

We believe this because we have a God who has a fine eye for detail, a God to whom a small gesture like the giving of a cup of water is not altogether lost. 'It shall by no means lose its reward,' is what he says of whatever small contribution we make towards the growing good of the world (Matthew 10:42). A thing done in his name is somehow touched by his presence, is transformed into a sacrament where the poor is God-become-our-neighbour, the person we feed and clothe and visit (Mark 9:41; Matthew 25:34-46). What looks like a drop of good in a bucket of evil will somehow endure to the end, not unremembered by a God who sees all things.

Also, the work of Christ tells us that a new order has come into being, incipient and as yet incomplete, but nevertheless real and powerful. The powers of the age to come has invaded human history, surprising us into a sense of its presence when something like the Berlin Wall falls down or a monolithic power like Marcos crumbles in a few days of unarmed siege.

So this we believe: a Kingdom of justice and righteousness has begun, and it is making its way into people's lives and denting structures that continue to oppress and dehumanize. Such work is seldom done in the corridors of power nor in the halls of the great. Often it is in the many small acts of integrity and goodness that many faceless men and women do every day, believing that behind the face of an evil that is strong is an unseen good that is stronger, even when it wears the face of weakness. It is this daily practice of hope which keeps most of us going, keeping the monsters at bay as humbly and powerfully we get caught up in kingdom fire and the stubborn grace that shines at the heart of existence.

LARGE-SCALE TRANSFORMATION TAKES SMALL STEPS

XIII
THE PRACTICE OF RADICAL HOPE
"Can these Bones Live?"

It must have been an awful sight. A valley full of dry bones, so dry the air must have crackled and rattled with them, spread itself before Ezekiel's eyes in a vision (Ezekiel 37:1-14). Before this desiccated wasteland, he was tested with a question, "Can these bones live?" Unable to imagine the possibility of life among such fossils, he hemmed and hawed, "O Lord God, thou knowest."

Ezekiel was not entirely unbelieving. Tucked in a corner of his mind he knew that God somehow knew the answer to that question, and could do something about it if he wanted to. The sight overwhelmed him enough, however, to feel doubtful about venturing an estimate of the situation.

Like Ezekiel, I sometimes feel the same tentativeness when faced with the desolate sense of defeat people feel about the monsters of our social experience. Poverty, debt, the land problem, coups and crime and militarism and never-ending corruption — all these tend to make us feel helpless and powerless, unable to believe things can change. We retreat into our own little corner of life barely able to survive, manning the ramparts of our own fragile hold on what is left of sanity and decency in this country. Filipinos everywhere feel a kind of inner capitulation, a surrender to the baser, poorer aspects of our socio-psychological makeup as a people — politicians whittling down social justice initiatives to accommodate powerful interests, destitute parents offering their own children to pedophiles and the flesh trade, soldiers protecting their own in defiance of a higher call to state loyalty and retributive justice, figures from the old regime returning, not to get shot like Romania's Caecescu, but to brazenly run for office and regain a foothold in the new order of things.

Ezekiel beholding a mass of dry bones is about the sort of sensation one feels watching the bustling crowds and scenes of Manila — a city without sufficient light or water or fuel, where streets are packed with buses and jeepneys bursting with human arms and legs flailing

99

out of windows and doors. It is a city under constant threat of the politics of terror, prostrate before corruption and lawlessness, tottering under the weight of the teeming poor and mountains of refuse and ash heaps, a city of garish lights and dark alleys rife with menace, reeking with blood and tears and the smell of vaporous vended flesh mixed with the stench of sewage, cheap scent and urine. It is said that when Jesus sees a crowd, he is moved with compassion for them. When I see a crowd, I can only wonder, "Can these bones live?"

Oddly enough, Ezekiel was to know the answer to that question by doing two curious things: one, talking to those very bones(!) and two, talking to the wind(!). "Prophesy to these bones, and say to them, 'O dry bones, hear the word of the Lord.'" The command must have stopped Ezekiel in his tracks. It is hard enough talking to an audience with hungry stomachs, distracted by the urgent pangs of the need for survival. It is impossible folly to talk to bones that have shriveled up, dried up skeletons hardly connected joint to joint. But then Ezekiel prophesied as he was commanded, and then there was a noise, and a rattling, and the bones came together, bone to bone, and flesh and skin covered them.

But there was no breath in them. So then again he was told, "Prophesy to the breath, prophesy, son of man, and say to the breath, 'Thus says the Lord God: Come from the four winds, O breath, and breathe upon these slain, that they may live.'"

To both commands, Ezekiel dutifully responds, "So I prophesied..." The bones quickened, and came to life. God explains that "these bones are the whole house of Israel," the exiles in Babylon who have lost hope of ever coming back to their native land. Their despondency at this time parallels that of people today who, submerged in hopeless poverty, cannot believe that things can ever be better. "Our bones are dried up, and our hope is lost," say the despairing exiles in Babylon, a disconsolate cry that echoes in the depths of our own souls as we see the general dejection of those who suffer.

Those of us who are in the business of changing society need to recognize that hopelessness happens in that part of people where God alone can go. That Christ was once dead reminds us that the forces of evil are strong; dark despair can overcome us in that place where the battle between hope and dissillusionment is waged. Often our bones dry up before the sheer intransigence of the forces that thwart our best efforts. The Cross means that all those good and great things we were going to do to forge a future for our people are going to run aground before the hardness of ancient wrongs.

Yet that Christ has risen also reminds us that at the center of power in this world is a force that breaks the tombs open and brings life: "Behold, I will open your graves, and raise you from your graves, O my people and I will bring you home into the land of Israel...And I will put my Spirit within you, and you shall live, and I will place you in your own land. Then you shall know that I, the Lord, have spoken, and I have done it, says the Lord."

Dejected Israel will rise, their spirits restored to vigour and life. A distraught nation crushed by foreign powers and bowed down by the experience of exile shall rise from the ash heap and go home. This is my own hope for our people — that a dispirited nation rendered dour and docile by centuries of oppression and degradation shall finally find within themselves the liberating resource of him who is able to make dry bones live.

As for those of us who sometimes feel stretched in our capacity to believe our own vision, our hope that Christ will come again strengthens our resolve to continue doing what we need to do against all odds — for the coming of the King is an imminent threat to evil, a thing of dread to those who have suicidally allied themselves with forces of darkness. What seems like never-ending wrong will cease, and always there is this threat of the return of the King who was and is to come.

So when we falter and are asked, "Can these bones live?" we cannot help but say 'yes' this side of Ezekiel, for

Christ has died,
Christ has risen,
and Christ will come again.

CONCLUSION
Kingdom Now – Living in the Age to Come

There's a rumor astir
that the woods are sold
and the purchaser
soon comes
(to transform
his fallen creation...)
    Rumor Unverified...
    Can you Confirm?

– Robert Penn Warren

For centuries the rumor has persisted.

In the half-light, among the shadows, men and women huddle and incline their heads to one another. The woods are sold, it is whispered. There is a new master. The reign of the Dark Lord is soon to be over. We need no longer stagger under the iron rule of his power.

Many have been killed and maimed for this sort of rumour-mongering. But no one has been able to put a stop to it. For though the earth is dark still and the woods are thick, sometimes, when one has the eye for it, the sky is seen through the trees, and light falls and shimmers on a patch of grass. The leaves rustle and a fever runs through the trees. A new world is coming, runs the tale. The earth, trembling, waits with eager longing.

It takes a lot of imagination to believe this rumour.

For one thing, it is asking us to believe that in that supreme act of weakness — the cross — a transfer of power had taken place. The strong man had been overthrown. A stronger man had disarmed him, had rendered him toothless, and had cast him out of the centre of power by which the world is ruled: "Now is the judgment of this world...now shall the ruler of this world be cast out..." (John 12:31).

These are huge claims for an event that in the eyes of the world is of little consequence: the death of an obscure Galilean whose very brief career was ended by an outburst of popular disfavour.

103

Just as in a fairy tale so much hangs on a kiss, a password or an answer to a riddle, we are told that on the cross, the life of the world hung on a thread. It was not with a massing of armies, with the flash and clanging of steel on steel that the fate of the world was decided. It was with a few nails and a tree, and the blood of a man who to all appearances looked quite unheroic, the sort who would not handle a sword and had none of the lordly air and martial spirit of the better Caesars.

There is a touch of magic in this. We are face to face with a story in which a door may open out into a strange new world, a frog may turn into a handsome prince and the rocks and trees into a palaceful of dancing spirits. We are being asked to enter a world of signs, where the pouring of blood is as good as the deed itself: the wresting of a groaning creation from the cruel hands of the evil one.

The key that would open up the world has been found. Where once there seemed to be no exit — a tap, a gentle push, and the trap door opens — and oh, the sight of flowers and sunlight!

This, roughly, is what the cross must mean to us in times when it is hard to believe that things can be any better. Many of us hobble through this life with the deep sense that nothing can be done about the cruel powers over us. There is the feeling that we are caught up in a monstrous network of evil, that now, more than ever, the world is reeling from the heavy-handed grip of forces much darker than before.

It is true that power structures continue to sprawl like subhuman monsters, often blind to human need. Evil seems more and more entrenched and more and more organized. In the Philippines especially, the subject of government is like a page out of Kafka. We feel we are somehow on trial for something, but there is no one to address our case to, no power to appeal to for a measure of justice or clarity. Poverty is like a thorn in the flesh: you wish it would go away but it is always there, staring hard. The best-laid plans of mice and men break and fail before the stubborn hardness of diseased social habits. Yet it is in the face of all this that we are being asked to believe that the reign of the true King has truly begun, that a 'new world' has entered human history and is making its mark on the monolith of powers oppressing humanity.

There is a decisiveness, a valiant finish to the work of Christ that allows us to believe that while evil seems strong and highly organized, it is in fact in its death throes. The Dragon is finished. It may fling and flail its arms wildly, crushing anyone within reach. But this is but the wild and nasty ragings of a dying beast. It is reeling from the pain of a wound that is fatal, and though it may try to hide under a show of invincible strength, this is its last act. It won't be long till the curtain falls and it is cast once for all into the nether gloom.

This is the root of our confidence in addressing ourselves to power structures. The powers that stand behind them have been defeated. The Stone is breaking the image, the great and terrible might of the kingdoms of this world (Daniel 2:44-45).

Part of the despair over political questions springs from the sense of futility we feel over our ability to change social structures. The Church, we say, is such a straggling minority to take upon Herself the task of changing society.

This overlooks the fact that the powers of the Kingdom are already present. The Kingdom is not entirely future, a sudden invasion from outer space at the end of time. It is here, leavening history in a powerful way.

While it is wrong to say that 'the world is getting better and better,' it is also wrong to say that 'the world is getting worse and worse.' It may be that the advance of technology has intensified the sense that evil has grown monolithic. But let us not be deceived. It is the dragon making a last desperate assault. For time is running out on it while the mustard seed is growing, hot and rich within and among us.

It is of course very hard to believe this. One reason is that we have a very short view of history. We are told that 2,000 years ago, something not quite continuous with the old order broke into our history and began a quiet, small work of burrowing deep into the fabric of a socio-economic structure built on the backs of slaves. "The axe is laid at the root of the tree," said John the Baptist (Matthew 3:10) but no one understood the nature of the crisis that the carpenter from Nazareth had brought. He was hanged from suspicions of being subversive of Caesar, but no evidence of rabble-rousing or conspiracy with the insurgent Zealots could be presented. It was only later, when the smoke rose from the ruins of the fallen Empire, that the threatening nature of his brand of politics became clear.

The church set the stage for a free-flowing social traffic that cut across barriers of race, sex and economic class, a blurring of boundaries that eventually weakened a society premised on privilege and exhausted by its own dissipations. It presented an alternative community in which a new social ethic may be realized. While not directly addressing political questions, it challenged the structures upon which inequalities were based. Today, centuries later, we are still feeling the shock waves of what it means to take seriously the ethics of the Kingdom that Jesus inaugurated. Christianity announced the coming of a new order, the fallout of which has left a trail of discarded institutions that have given way to the strength of its transforming power.

Quite unseen, the leavening power of the Kingdom continues to work against the forces of witchcraft, superstition, disease and ignorance in remote minority cultures. For all of its faults, the modern missionary movement remains an instrument in this confrontation. Meanwhile, Third World Christians are waking up to the radical nature of the watered-down Christianity that has been handed down to them. The pressure to respond to the overwhelming fact of poverty and oppression has led to a rediscovery of the cosmic proportions of salvation, and an increasing concern to see the strong presence of the Kingdom in the ruling of power structures.

The point is that the Kingdom has made an impact. Here, in this bent earth, it has been growing and releasing men and women from the bondage of sin and oppression. It takes a long-range vision to appreciate the power and the reality of its presence.

To be sure, this is not exactly the world picture being shown to us. If we listen to the media, the picture is that of unrelenting lawlessness. There is very little of the grace that is making its way into the lives of individuals and of nations.

It is sad that we are taken in by the unrelieved blackness of contemporary history, a thing that in our better moments we know to be merely 'shadows' in the language of Ellul, a phantasmal concoction of government offices, demagogues and reporters. In many ways, we have lost our sense of 'primary history' — the primitive, raw experience of life as we know it. The world around us may be heart-breaking, but our instincts tell us that even among the poor, the strong grace of God prevails. Even though there is no horde of reporters, no cameras clicking.

The face of the Kingdom may seem insignificant, but this is no sign of weakness; it is in fact an indication of the strength of God that he is prepared to be weak. For some mysterious reason, the lion is also a lamb, and the Kingdom is as leaven, a quiet, hidden presence.

It is part of the irony of existence that when the most decisive event in the history of the world was about to take place, the disciples slept. Like us, they did not have the eyes to see the great hand of God in the movement of the small.

In spite of the story of David and Goliath, most of us would rather trust in chariots. Power structures remain unclaimed territory, mostly because, like the Israelites, we easily get intimidated by sheer size. Our grasshopper sense of smallness inhibits us from calling the power structures to account.

There is no doubt that we are seeing in our time an intensification of the crisis between the seed of the Woman and the seed of the Serpent. Technology, the market and other institutions are being organized behind one or the other. While we must renounce worldly uses of power, we must understand that power will be used for evil if it is not being used for good. Implicit in our commitment to uphold institutions is the confidence that power may be used for good. While power may corrupt, it is not inherently corrupting.

It is important to grasp that we do not live in an evil order, but in a corrupted one. The world is still good, it is our Father's world and the Son bought it back at such costly price to himself. While we yearn for final deliverance from the corruption of the present age, we do not renounce it as without hope of achieving present good. A breach has been made, the powers of the new world are breaking in.

So let us not be daunted. The powers of the Beast may surround and rail against us; it may be that we seem small before flashy displays of strongman power. But that should not bother us; the beast is dying, and fallen, fallen is Babylon the Great. The kingdoms of this world are passing. There is no need to be impressed.

The world will falter and break around us. It cannot be helped. But let us have an eye for the mustard seed, for the signs of the new age. It will not be long till the King comes, in a lightning flash and a cloudburst, a 'stun of jewels.' In the meantime, let us prepare the way for the coming world, and once again hear the Church Father Cyprian as he sees the crumbling of the Roman Empire and brings these words to God's people: "Let us stand upright amid the ruins of the world, and not lie on the ground as those who have no hope."